**profit
planning
and
control**

PROFIT
PLANNING
AND
CONTROL

T. S. McAlpine, AACCA, ACWA

BUSINESS BOOKS LIMITED
London

First published 1969

© THOMAS SOMERVILLE MCALPINE 1969

SBN 220.79894.x

This book has been set in 11 on 14 pt Times Roman,
printed in England by Hazell Watson & Viney Ltd,
Aylesbury, Bucks, for the publishers, Business Books Limited
(registered office: 180 Fleet Street, London EC4); publishing
offices: Mercury House, Waterloo Road, London SE1

MADE AND PRINTED IN GREAT BRITAIN

contents

illustrations

1 product policy, marketing and design

Economic growth is the ultimate measure of the success of a business and this is generally reflected in three ways.

An expanding volume of sales through an increase in market demand. An expanding market is essential for economic growth.

Increasing sales through an increasing share of the market; a fair indication that the business is improving its competitive position.

Increasing profits which reflect not only the increasing volume of sales but also, in the longer term, a better return on the capital employed. This indicates the efficient application of the resources of the business: men, materials, money and management.

Success requires a careful consideration of the best contribution a business can make having regard to its particular skills and resources as measured against its opportunities and the outside forces. This requires a critical appraisal of the business to see factually what it is and what it should be. In a dynamic and rapidly changing environment this appraisal has to be regularly undertaken and effectively implemented for a business to prosper. In the development stage of a business these considerations are particularly important to ensure a rational product pattern that will promote economic growth.

Contrary to what may be expected it is not easy to see a business as it is, that is to see it steady and to see it whole, and it can be difficult to decide what it should be. These considerations raise two questions: 'who within the organization has the specific task of making these decisions?' and 'what is the concept of a business?'

In the large business there will probably be a planning committee to advise the chief executive in these matters but this is unlikely in the average-sized business. Generally the chief executive will be responsible for making these decisions but he should be ably supported by the other executives in reaching his decision.

In most companies there are four or more major functions including marketing, technical (which includes product design, research and development), production and finance, each in charge of an executive reporting direct to the chief executive. This can provide the organizational framework for policy decisions if the executives can see the business in its total perspective and not only from the functional viewpoint.

Acting independently, as is too often the case, each executive will only see the business through his particular function and it can generally be expected that the views of different executives will differ on what the business is and what it should be. In fact their individual views and interests will usually conflict; for example, the marketing executive may favour an extensive product range as a means of maximizing sales whereas the production executive would like to restrict the range to the products which provide long production runs and low costs; the marketing executive will press for substantial product inventories to ensure quick deliveries to customers whereas the finance executive will be concerned with minimizing the investment in inventories; and these are only a few of the differences that generally exist.

It is only when the executives think and act as a management team that a co-ordinated and balanced view is likely to emerge and the business be in a fair way to determine what its future should be.

Management sophistication of this order does not happen but has to be created, and it is the primary responsibility of the chief executive to create it. Established management processes operating through corporate policies and planned objectives will provide the basis.

product policy

The products that a company makes decide the fundamental nature of the business at any point of time. It is only through its products that a business can determine its customers, its markets, its competitors, and the type and size of organization necessary for its operation. The product sets the limit of opportunity for the economic growth of a business. Product policies are the focal point of business strategy and a business can only be viable and progressive when it clearly sees the products that will provide the required sales income for at least three years ahead.

A customer only sees a business through its product; its quality, appearance, price and availability, and sometimes its reputation. The outstanding feature of the successful business is that its products are amongst the leaders in their particular field. The introduction by Wilkinson a few years ago of a stainless steel razor blade was a good example of the impact an outstanding product can have on a market.

A sound product policy is the starting point in building a successful business.

Alfred P. Sloan Junior in his book 'My years with General Motors' said that one of the most significant factors in the evolution of the corporation was the framing of a product policy. It laid the foundation which transformed an ordinary business to its present position as the largest business in the world. It was a product policy admirably implemented that created the Ford empire. Henry Ford cherished the idea of making a car for the masses at a time when it was an expensive luxury only within the reach of a few wealthy people and he realised his ambition through the famous 'T' model which was the start of large volume, low price production.

A sound product policy is a means of ensuring that a business is competent to produce and market the products included in its range, that is to produce a product that is better than most and as good as the best. There should be an expanding market for the products and the business should be capable of achieving a sales volume that will permit economic operation. In this connection the small business can be as efficient as the large business providing it chooses the products appropriate to its size and realises that it cannot make the variety or complexity of product that is only suited to large scale operation.

A business can fail when it engages in a product that is too complex for its size and resources. The sales volume and consequently the sales income being restricted, expenditure has to be dictated by what the business can afford and not by what the product demands. This is a case of the sales volume being too low to support economic operation and this is frequently expressed in two ways: the design, research and development expenditure is inadequate to produce the class of product that will command market status, and production costs are excessive because the low volume cannot justify the production methods and the plant investment necessary for economic operation.

A progressive business must be sensitive to outside forces in formulating and implementing its product policy. It must understand the industry in which it operates and must be informed on competitive and market changes which can influence its sales volume, and on technological developments which can have an impact on its products.

A manufacturer of solid-fuel boilers, for example, is not only in competition with manufacturers of the same product but with all manufacturers of heating appliances. This is an important consideration in formulating and implementing a product policy.

Technological developments which may influence the products of a business can generally be detected in advance. The danger lies in underestimating the effects of these developments and some companies have failed for this reason.

The attitude of the manufacturers of steam locomotives to the diesel engine was a flagrant example of discounting a technological development. They refused to believe that the steam locomotive was outdated and when it became a fact their resources were too depleted to transfer to another business. This happened in both America and Britain.

the concept of a business

The concept of a business embraces products and markets with sales volume and resources as other important considerations. Some companies express the concept of the business through their product policy and market strategy. This is a rational procedure for products with a long life and expanding markets. But many products have a comparatively short life cycle and in these conditions it can be more appropriate to think and plan beyond the present product policy to provide a more reliable and durable operating basis.

A study of the most successful companies shows that they have generally one characteristic in common and that is a clearly defined concept of the business largely influenced by the chief executive. Two good examples of this influence are Alfred P. Sloan Junior of General Motors and Thomas J. Watson Junior of International Business Machines; and in Britain, Lord Stokes of Leyland Motors.

It is the policy of some companies to purposely widen the concept and the characteristics of the business beyond its product policy. Notwithstanding its leading position in the computer field, International Business Machines does not regard itself as being in the computer business or even in the data processing business. The concept of the business is 'Our business is the creation of machines and methods to help find solutions to the increasingly complex problems of business, government, science, space exploration, education, medicine, and nearly every other area of human endeavour'. This calls for a different class of personnel with different training and another type of sales organisation and product policy.

The strategic concept of Du Pont is expressed in the slogan 'Better things for better living through chemistry'. The company spends considerable sums on research and development as a policy and achieves its object through a steady stream of new products. Nevertheless the concept of a business for most companies must, in the short term at least, be translated into concrete terms; it must project a product policy and product lines that will take care of the sales income for the next three to five years.

The concept of a business maps out the road to progress for each particular business. A business without the guidelines of a concept and a product policy cannot be fully effective and is likely to attract the wrong products or to divide its concentration. This is reflected by the number of companies who justify certain unprofitable product lines by explaining that they make a contribution to overheads. The fact is that in most cases these products should never have been introduced.

marketing

The success of a business is largely determined by finding the right answers to the questions 'what products and what markets'. The aim and purpose of a product policy are to provide the right answers, but their implementation is primarily the concern of marketing and product design and these two functions must be closely linked.

Marketing is essential to ensure that a product realises its full sales potential. It is also essential to provide the intelligence that will keep the business sensitive and resilient to outside forces.

It is a fundamental of marketing that the goods to be produced should aim at satisfying the wants of the customer and not simply the needs of the manufacturer. It is frequently implied, and this is often quoted as a justification for marketing orientation, that the manufacturer does not study the customer.

The fact is that every business executive knows or very soon learns that customer needs dominate the purpose of the business. Where a manufacturer fails to satisfy customer demand there is usually another reason.

The operation of a business would be simplified and the risks substantially reduced if a customer was articulate in his wants. The task that faces a business is not simply to interpret the wants of the customer but to anticipate them. Innovation is the key to satisfying customer wants and this has its attendant risks of success or failure. No company however successful or experienced can be free from this risk. Leading car manufacturers who are probably better placed than most companies to know what the customer wants can never be certain that a new model will be a success. For example, Ford in 1957–8 introduced the highly publicised Edsel car which had all the attributes of success but did not get the market response. The customer expresses his preference in the choice of the products available and to study the customer one must study what he buys. The kitchen which was once the workshop of the domestic dwelling is now the showpiece. This revolution was started through manu-facturers innovations which obtained a ready response from the customer.

In considering a new product or an updated version of an existing product it is a recognized practice, dependent upon the product and management sophistication, for the marketing division to submit a product specification. This specification will generally detail the standards set by the market and will largely reflect the developments of the leading competitors. The value of such a specification often lies in its interpretation of market restraints thus ensuring that the product will conform and that serious errors of judgement will be avoided. The selling price obtainable will be quoted together with an estimate of the volume of sales. Where a new product is involved it is usual to estimate the annual sales over a period of three years and where it is a feasible project authority is given to develop the design on paper and to submit drawings and other information for costing the product. If the cost of the product shows a satisfac-tory profit permission is given to manufacture prototypes and if no unforseen factors arise this is followed by an order to manufacture a number for market tests before embarking on a production programme.

One of the mistakes that is not uncommon in business is to assume that a product which has proved itself in one market is equally suitable for another market. An example will illustrate the point.

A business manufacturing plant for outside construction work had standardised its design for the home market but made to order for the export market. Export sales were 60 per cent of total sales. In the immediate post-war period it was decided to make only the standard product for home and export markets. For several years this policy was successful and output and sales increased substantially. Then export sales declined and stocks increased considerably and the overseas agents reported that it was due to a trade recession. The management consultants who were advisers to the company did not accept this explanation and three experienced sales engineers armed with carefully prepared questionnaires were sent to contact agents and visit actual sites. The results were conclusive. The product, basically designed for the home market, was not robust enough for the working conditions abroad, spare parts were not readily available and competitors were supplying equipment to the particular requirements of the customer. It was apparent that the original policy could only operate during a period of scarcity, a position that could have been foreseen had the company taken the logical precaution of studying the requirements of the market.

One of the factors that is assuming more importance in an age of accelerating change is the life cycle of the product. This is a logical reaction when the life cycle is shortening in relation to the time required to design and develop a new product. Some products have a relatively short life; for example, toys and fashion clothes. Other products have a comparatively long life but only if the design is updated at regular intervals. It is important to know the life cycle of a product and the stage it has reached; first by ascertaining when a replacement product or an updated model will be required; secondly to decide on sales promotion tactics dependent upon whether the product has a growth potential or has passed its peak; thirdly to adjust selling price to give a flexible sales basis.

Some industries now realise that the introduction of new models periodically is not confined to the automobile trade. A leading supplier of domestic appliances noticed a marked decline in the sales of one of its products and found that it was due to a new model introduced by a competitor. This forced the company to make a closer study of the market. The new model was no better but customers believed that being a later model it was more advanced. This forced the company to formulate a policy on new models.

A business cannot operate successfully without attempting to measure quantitatively the potential sales of its products in present and future markets. Regardless of size a business must have all the ingredients necessary within its marketing organization to fulfil the particular demands of the product. The smaller business will not employ as many people as the larger business but it will generally have the same activities, for example, establishing distribution channels, providing market intelligence and competitor profiles, sales promotion and selling.

Products can be broadly classified into three categories: consumer goods, consumer durables and industrial. There are, of course, countless varieties within each category. Sales representatives will generally be employed in all three categories but the importance attached to them will vary. In some cases advertising will supplement the efforts of the sales representatives and in other cases the emphasis will be on advertising with sales representation an adjunct to it. Some companies employ trained sales representatives with no technical baekground while others employ technical representatives or sales engineers. The demands of the product and the market as interpreted by the individual business will decide the pattern.

The interpretation of the demands of the product and deciding the most appropriate selling methods are not simple as marketing, unlike the other functions, has few guidelines or established principles. The effectiveness of sales organizations can, therefore, vary considerably, and a methodical study of requirements and careful planning can have a marked influence on performarce.

It is probably in the industrial field that technical representation, or sales engineering, has the strongest pull and the greatest influence on sales. The leading position of International Business Machines is a good illustration of the benefits that can be obtained from well trained and competent sales engineers. It can be expected however that the technical representative of the future will differ from his counterpart of today in that his duties and outlook will not be confined only to representing the company to the customer but he will be 'the eyes and ears' of the business. He will be trained to report objectively on all matters within his territory which influence the business, and he will be familiar with market surveys, product acceptance and share of the market, performance of competitors, and product and market developments.

Sales management will also be more effective and facts as opposed to opinions will be the guiding principles. The best practices, largely confined at present to the more progressive companies, will be more widely known and applied. For example:

An annual quota for each sales representative. This will normally be done within the framework of an annual sales budget for the company. The performance of the representative will be measured each month by comparing the orders obtained from his territory against his sales quota.

Special attention to the large customer. It is not unusual to find in many companies that some 20 per cent of the customers account for about 80 per cent of the total sales. The calls of the representative on the large customer should be supplemented periodically, once or twice per year, by a visit of the area manager, or the sales manager.

Customer record cards. A record card kept for each customer, or the more important customer, showing the sales record and the date of each call by the representative. Some companies arrange for the sales records to be reviewed quarterly and any showing a marked decline are noted for action.

Assessing the required number of sales representatives. Some companies, perhaps the minority, base this on a factual appraisal. An estimate of the number of actual and potential customers is made for each territory. These are then classified into three or four groups according to the actual or potential sales and the frequency of call decided for each group, for example monthly, quarterly or six-monthly. The number of calls that a representative can be expected to make within a given period related to the number of calls that have to be made will provide the basis for deciding the number of representatives required.

Record of calls made. A record is maintained showing the number of calls made by each representative. A monthly report may be prepared showing the number of calls made by each representative and the cost per call or other significant data.

Perhaps the most significant development in marketing will be in the wider and more intensive application of planned objectives which will encompass products, markets and volume of sales, and will promote a closer study of marketing methods and marketing organizations.

Many of the big decisions in business will be based on information provided by the marketing organization and the requirements will increase in volume and complexity.

The problems in fact-finding and decision-making will not be eliminated but more efficient techniques for dealing with them will certainly emerge, particularly in the factual interpretation of the information available.

Relevant information does not of itself produce the facts. Much information may be collected but few facts may emerge from it. It is the old story of 'sorting the wheat from the chaff'.

The demand for information usually precedes the ability of the organisation to provide it.

Few major decisions can be made with all the facts available; there are usually some significant factors that cannot be determined.

Decision-making is in the end a matter of personal judgement with, at best, the risk narrowed down to a few alternatives.

The conditions that faced a chemical company can be quoted as a typical case. One of the chemicals manufactured by the company had the largest share of the home market and was sold in many countries abroad. There was strong international competition but the ceiling price for each market was fairly closely defined.

The production plant of the optimum size to give the minimum production cost per unit of product required an investment of approximately three-quarters of a million pounds and as the plant was designed around a particular method of manufacture it was not adaptable to a change of method. A catalyst was used in producing the chemical and as this was the largest element in cost there was the constant risk that a competitor would develop an alternative and cheaper method of production. Meanwhile, of course, the company was striving for an alternative method.

The marketing organization followed the normal pattern as shown in Appendix 1. The company had reached the point where it had to consider additional production capacity to meet an expanding demand in the export markets. The question was what size of plant, or plants, and where to locate them. The company had no reliable information on the export markets situation and its marketing organization could not contribute anything of value since it was domestically orientated. The export agents submitted their views but had no supporting data to show the size of the markets actual and potential, or the probable rate of growth; nor could they state the company's share of the market.

The company had to obtain precise information on the markets since it was confronted with a two-fold objective of (a) avoiding any loss of actual or potential sales and (b) minimizing the investment in additional plant since it was not aware of the progress of competitors in finding an alternative method of production.

product design

Technological developments and increasing competition necessitate a much closer liaison between marketing and product design. This product/market integration, which has its starting point in the product specification and a forecast of sales and selling price, provides the guidelines for design and a reasonable assurance that the product will conform with the requirements of the market.

Product/market integration is indispensible in the efficient operation of a business. Around 1957 American car manufacturers designed a small car for the economy-minded customer who wanted a low-priced car with low running costs. Contradictorily it became evident that the customer wanted better interior appointments, equipment such as automatic transmission and power steering, and the range of models and styles that were available in the regular cars. More than half the sales of the Corvair, made by General Motors, featured automatic transmission. This is a good example of product/market integration.

Design and production must also be closely integrated. It is essential that the components and the finished product are made to the required standards, and that the design should aim at simplicity of manufacture and avoid refinements that increase production costs but add nothing to the performance or the value of the product.

In general there are few products that are designed as well as they should be both from the viewpoint of the customer and the business. Inferior and cheap are not synonymous in product design as almost invariably the resultant product costs more and not less to produce. In many companies the authority of the design department is unchallenged provided that it takes cognisance of the product specification submitted by the marketing division. The production division is given the opportunity to comment on the design before it is finalised but their remarks are usually confined to particular points of difficulty in manufacture where concessions are necessary.

Some of the more obvious shortcomings in product design are: specifying finer limits than necessary, thus adding to the number of production operations; specifying a non-standard part which has to be made specially instead of the standard part of a supplier; using a variety of sections and quality of materials instead of developing a few standards that would generally apply. In recent years value engineering and value analysis have obviated many of the weaknesses in product design.

A design department can operate more efficiently when guidelines are established. Guiding principles should be laid down and standards formulated and the whole should be brought within the framework of written procedures.

One feature of product design that presents a challenge and an opportunity to the designer is standardization. It is not in the design of standard products that the real opportunity arises as here the principles are well known and generally observed but in the standardization of the parts of a product which cannot itself be standardized. It is surprising how little attention is given to the standardization of components in the non-standard product and yet in every case where this is earnestly studied worthwhile results are generally obtained. Standardization can usually be an attitude of mind as the following example shows. In one factory standard products accounted for 90 per cent of the output and product B, a non-standard product, for the other 10 per cent. Commenting on product B the chief designer said that it was a standard product with modifications to suit the customer and every component had been standardized where practicable. In another factory product B was the only manufacture and here the designer commented that it was a non-standard product with certain common parts. The product had not been studied from the viewpoint of standardization and the common parts had been standardized because they were too obvious to miss.

There are two common factors that react against good design. First, where the organization of the department in its skills and in the number employed is dictated by the economics and not the logic of the situation. Where two companies A and B are designing the same product and A can reasonably expect to sell twice as many as B it follows that A can afford to spend more on design than B with probably better results. Secondly, where an arbitrary time limit is imposed for designing a product as dictated by the situation and not by the requirements of the product.

The design of the product, in conjunction with the volume of sales, basically fixes the cost of the product. Other factors may influence the cost but do not alter this basic principle; for example, the efficiency of production or the level of overheads can have a favourable or an unfavourable impact on cost but these are not basic characteristics.

summary: the total view

Planning is the key to the continuance and expansion of a business. It may be formal, systematic and factual, or it may be dictated by expediency and *ad hoc* decisions, and the results achieved will generally be in direct proportion to the thought, consideration and skill applied to it.

A business must be definite in what it is trying to do over the next two to five years and how it intends to do it, and the objectives must be supported by the necessary skills and resources. Effective planning requires a thorough knowledge and understanding of the business and of the industry in which it operates and an appreciation of the outside forces that influence its environment. It requires a business to organise its expectations and to develop programmes for their achievement.

Planning may be long or short term and both are generally necessary. Ideally there should only be one plan at any period of time, distinction being made in the time phasing of the different sections.

The basic factors, or elements, generally require long term planning, whereas the operating factors are essentially short term, usually a period of one year.

The basic elements are products and markets and stemming from them the volume of output. In most companies these must be long term considerations: designing and developing new products or updating the designs of existing products; extending markets or establishing new markets; enlarging the capacity of the production plant to cope with an increasing volume of sales.

The operating elements relate to current operations which are usually planned through the annual budget. The budget is primarily aimed at formulating a sales programme and fixing a sales quota for each product and each territory. From this the other budgets are formulated and finally expressed in terms of income, expenditure and profit. The one thing that an annual budget should do is to assign a definite responsibility to the marketing function through a sales programme and sales quotas. The annual budget may also fix a production programme but many companies are forced by circumstances to programme production on a shorter period, probably anything from two to six months. Generally, however, companies are prepared to submit letters of intent to suppliers stating their requirements for the year based on the information contained in the annual budget.

The planning of business objectives has to be positive in determining who should be responsible for planning and in setting up planning procedures. In large industrial concerns planning may be assigned to a planning committee but for the average-sized business this can probably be organized most effectively through a management committee comprising all or most of the top executives under the chairmanship of the chief executive.

Management decisions must be based on facts insofar as these are obtainable. Since the relevant information can only be obtained through question and answer it is important that the right questions are posed in order to obtain accurate and comprehensive answers. Where a major decision has to be made it is well worth preparing and approving a questionnaire before proceeding. In this connection there is a general need for improving data collection and the processing of information as an aid to better planning.

Business objectives begin with product/market strategy. Product plans are the foundation since the product sets the limits of opportunity for the survival and growth of the business. Products and markets must generally be considered together to ensure that the product is designed to the particular requirements of the market as interpreted and specified by the marketing division. Where there is market segmentation made up of two or more groups of customers who can be expected to respond differently to product features and price differentials, it is important to identify the particular segment for which the product is being designed. Associating the product with the market is the most precise operation in the management of a business; and the shotgun must give place to the rifle.

Product designers cannot design effectively in a vacuum; they must be guided by market demands and a close link must, therefore, be maintained between research, development, product design and marketing. There is a problem in interpreting market requirements as the user is not articulate in his demands. In many products the manufacturer has to be ahead of the customer in anticipating his requirements, and the marketing function in its specification of the product may be limited to stating what successful competitors are doing and emphasising certain features that must be avoided.

Product/market strategy should be expressed as a product policy, which for most industrial companies will decide the nature of the business for some years ahead and therefore, requires very careful consideration. It is the most important decision that the average company is called upon to make and it is an issue that cannot be left to chance if a business wants to survive and prosper.

2 plan of organization

The object in planning the organization is to create a team that will effectively implement the policies, objectives and directions of management. Organizing is a part of the managing process and the organization must be designed for efficient business performance.

It is essential for the average business to see how and where its income will be obtained in the next three to five years. It must see this in terms of products, markets and volume of sales, and this outlook will determine the type of organization that is required.

An organization is formed basically by assigning work to people and it involves the analysis and grouping of activities into functions and then into positions, and the selection of the right persons for these positions. The organization framework is persons, positions, authority, relations, and procedures. The steps in planning the organization may be broadly classified as:

Functional Analysis: analysing and grouping the activities into functions.

Positions: analysing the function into sub-functions and positions.

Duties and Authority: determining the duties and authority appropriate to each position.

Job Appraisal: analysing and specifying the requirements of the position.

Personnel Appraisal: assessing and matching individual qualifications against the job specification.

Co-ordination: establishing functional relations for efficient performance.

functional analysis

No two business concerns are alike and this will be reflected in the organization. The ideas and outlook of management, the type of business and the capabilities of the personnel, will all influence the type of organization. There are no set rules for analysing and grouping activities into functions but there are certain guide lines which can aid decisions. The functions common to most business operations are: marketing, technical (which includes design, research and development), manufacturing, purchasing, industrial relations and accounting and financing. The importance attached to each of these functions can vary considerably between one business and another. Purchasing and industrial relations in particular can show wide divergencies from being under the control of the works manager to being represented at board level. There can be wide variations too in the activities contained in a particular function and only a special study of the needs of the business will give the right grouping for efficient performance.

In general too little attention is given to the grouping and sub-grouping of activities considering their importance in the operation of the business. The needs and aims of the business have to be carefully studied as the basis for planning the organization. The organization should be built around the function and not around individuals, and all the activities necessary for the proper performance of a function should be contained in that function. For example, market research and advertising would be included in the marketing function, and production planning and control would be part of the manufacturing function. A functional chart is sometimes prepared to show the grouping of activities and an example is given in Appendix 2.

Most organizations are the result of growth. A business starts in a small way and in the beginning the authority is vested in one or two individuals each performing two or more functions. As the business grows more persons are appointed and functions are delegated. One of the weaknesses that can emerge is that the process of delegation does not match expansion. A person may control two or more functions and as the volume of work increases he is given one or two assistants. As growth continues this method becomes ineffective and some concerns are slow to realise that a planned organization is needed. This condition is not confined to the small developing business as various stages of growth invariably necessitate reorganization.

In planning the organization each function is defined without regard to personnel and when the organization structure is determined individuals are selected to fill the positions.

positions and authority

Authority confers the right to command subordinates to perform certain duties. The authority assigned to a position will depend upon the importance attached to it by the management and should be related to the duties and responsibilities of the position and the class of decisions that are inherent in it. The place of the position within the organization will be defined by stating who reports to whom. This can best be covered by a statement in writing of the responsibilities of the position as shown in Appendix 3.

The allocation of duties and responsibilities is a matter for careful consideration for without proper planning the odds are against building an efficient organization. There is no better illustration of this than to observe the importance attached to a foreman by various companies. In the days of F. W. Taylor, one of the early pioneers of scientific management, all the operations of a factory revolved around the foreman. Since then many of his duties have been taken over by specialist departments such as methods engineering, work study, production planning and control, inspection, and personnel management. Now the duties and responsibilities of the foreman are the direction and control of the workers to ensure that the department produces the required output of the required quality at the required time and at an economic cost. If the foreman does not do this who does? This is a measure of the importance of the job.

There are many companies where the status of the foreman is not commensurate with his responsibilities, perhaps because he is overshadowed by the specialist departments, and this can lead to a contradictory condition. The management, because it tends to downgrade the importance of the function, usually appoints a foreman who is below the standard really required, and when asked, perhaps by consultants, why more authority is not given to the position the answer quite often is that the man is not capable of carrying added responsibility.

There are several factors which make the function of a foreman important. He is the first line of management and he can be a dynamic factor in increasing productivity. He is at the point of production and all the directions and instructions from the top management downwards depend upon him for translation into efficient performance.

Likewise the directions of methods engineering, production planning and control, and other departments, are only plans on paper until they are co-ordinated and translated into physical reality by the foreman. Finally the majority of the employees in a business are under the direct control of foremen and this in itself makes the position important.

In general the shop supervisory function should be elevated, (a) as the best means at the disposal of management for increasing productivity, and (b) to relieve higher management of the necessity to make numerous decisions which could be better undertaken closer to the action stations.

Decentralization with co-ordinated control will be the future pattern of business operation. It will be inevitable as a means of relieving top management from detailed decisions and allowing it to concentrate on its major task of strategic planning. This implies more responsibility for shop supervision which in turn means that shop supervisors must be trained to meet the challenge of this emerging role. A foreman will be required to have a knowledge of methods engineering, work study application, production planning, industrial psychology and cost control, in conjunction with experience of factory operations and labour control.

The function of the foreman has been discussed at length because this can be a blind spot of management. The future trend will be for decisions to be made at the lowest possible level and close to the facts. This will require the training of personnel to enable them to make these decisions. This will have the two-fold effect of developing personnel and improving business performance.

job appraisal

It has to be decided which activities logically belong together for the best performance and to group them together into one function and sub-functions. The next step is to decide the different positions within a function and to determine the duties appropriate to each position. This is necessary for two reasons: first it defines the duties and responsibilities of the position and its place in the organisation, and secondly it provides a job specification as a basis for selecting the right person for the position.

personnel appraisal

This is an assessment of the qualifications of the individual as related to the requirements of the particular position. The job specification in defining the duties and responsibilities of the position permits an assessment to be made of the qualifications required to fill it.

In its recruitment of personnel and in its plan of organisation the aim of a business will be to fit the person to the job and not the job to the person. This is an ideal that cannot always be achieved. To ensure that standards of performance are not lowered by these conditions management must institute training programmes, planned objectives which define the performance required from each position, and procedures and standard practices which promote efficient operation.

co-ordination

It is necessary to co-ordinate the various functions for the fulfilment of a common objective, and the relation of one function to another must be established and defined in terms of inter-related services.

Activities can best be co-ordinated within a function but there are limits to the number of activities that can be contained within a single function. The qualification required for directing and controlling an extended function is one limiting factor and the span of control is another. It would be unusual, for example, to find an executive who could direct and control both marketing and manufacturing except in the smallest companies, and if it were possible it would not be desirable as there would be the problem of succession.

The span of control limits the activities that can be contained in a function since there is a limit to the number of persons who can report direct to the functional head. It is a fairly widespread belief that the number of persons reporting to a functional head should not exceed six or seven, but in practice this can vary considerably dependent upon the type of business and how smoothly and efficiently the organisation operates. In some companies as many as ten and eleven report direct with no ill-effects on the efficiency of the organization. The advantages of extending the span of control are that it reduces the number of management levels and shortens the line of communications.

There are three types of authority that are frequently referred to in connection with organization, namely line, function and staff. These can complicate organizational planning and co-ordination. Line authority gives the head the right to command his subordinates. Functional (or technical) authority gives the right to state how things will be done to departments not directly responsible to it. A typical example is the controller who has functional authority over all accounting procedures in the business. The staff activity normally carries out special investigations and makes reports and investigations. It operates in an advisory capacity without authority or jurisdiction over any other department.

decentralization and co-ordinated control

This is a form of organization that can be very effective when a business contains several distinctive units each a business in itself. Each unit is a separate operating division and is designed usually around certain products or group of products. The aim is to give the operating division the maximum autonomy and freedom to manage its own affairs within certain defined standards of performance against which its results can be measured. The operating division is fully accountable for its results which are generally measured by the profit earned.

The reconciliation of the conflicting elements of centralization or decentralization can be a problem—what to delegate and what to retain at central headquarters. Top management is in a difficult position in that it can delegate authority but cannot delegate responsibility. To fulfil its responsibility to the business, top management can only delegate authority when there are established standards against which to measure performance and a regular flow of information to show the performance achieved. Therefore, top management can only delegate authority when it can control performance, or, to put it another way, there cannot be decentralization without co-ordinated control.

Decentralization normally applies in conditions of autonomous divisions obviously because performance can be positively measured but there is no reason to believe that the principle should not be extended if the proper conditions are created: (a) standards for measuring performance and (b) regular information to show the performance achieved.

Decentralization is only necessary to the extent that management is prepared to delegate authority and this is conditioned by the various decisions that have to be made and the level at which they should be made. Bearing in mind the principle that decisions should preferably be made close to the action point and the facts, there is something to be said for the statement that 'decisions should be considered from the bottom upwards and not from the top downwards'.

Applying this principle the first consideration would be the decisions that should preferably be made at shopfloor level. This consideration would be based on an objective analysis without regard to the qualifications of existing personnel. Three important points can emerge from this analysis: first a statement of the decisions to be made in connection with shop operations; secondly a recommendation on the decisions that are within the authority of the foreman and those which should be made at a higher level; the final point is to decide if a foreman needs any particular training to give effect to the recommendations.

If this principle is applied progressively throughout the whole of the organization the decisions left to top management, apart from those major considerations which cannot be delegated, will be limited to those that should not be settled at a lower level. This is a factor of primary importance in business and management efficiency which will require more attention in the future than is given at present because management is regularly deciding issues which should be cleared at a lower level. This procedure presumes that the delegation of more authority is backed by the necessary control and that each level of management has the information to measure and control the performance of the next lower level for which it is responsible.

the personality of a business

A business like an individual has a personality: good, bad or indifferent. This personality evolves in a number of ways and sometimes extends over a long period. There are quite a few concerns operating today on the principles that were laid down by their founders more than fifty years ago. The spirit of an organization, the philosophy of a business, competent and outstanding management gifted with the happy knack of making common people do uncommon things, the class of personnel employed; these and many other things go to make up the personality of a business.

The personality of a business can have a tremendous impact on efficiency. Management, particularly new management, can draw strength and assurance from a business with a good personality, or be faced with a formidable task where there is a bad personality. It is a subtle point but nevertheless real and significant.

procedures and standards of performance

Procedures implement the organization. The functional grouping of activities shows the jobs that have to be done and the procedures show how they should be done. Standards provide the yardstick for measuring performance.

Some 80 to 90 per cent of the operations in a business are repetitive and therefore justify a careful study to determine the best methods of performing these routines. Some procedures will be spread over two or more functions and several departments and if properly planned and implemented can be an effective co-ordinating factor in the organization. Procedures should be in writing for the guidance of employees to ensure that they know the system and apply it properly. Experience shows that written procedures produce better results.

An organization cannot operate effectively without planned procedures. In the absence of established procedures problems arise and have to be settled at a higher level than is necessary because routine and non-routine matters are not clearly segregated, and the general outcome is that management at all levels is pre-occupied with detail to the exclusion of major considerations.

Once the procedures are established and standards of performance formulated the personnel required in relation to the work load can be determined. Standards of performance may be qualitative or quantitative or both. In a production department it is usual to have both standards: operational times as determined by the work study department through work measurement studies, and a quality or performance specification for the product.

There are several areas of a business for which quantitative standards are not generally determined, for example office sections, and here the personnel required is based on current and past experience. Periodically these areas can be studied to assess the work load in relation to the personnel employed.

There are two standards of performance which should apply in most industrial enterprises; the operating standard which only changes when the method is changed and the objective standard. Operational times and the product specification are examples of operating standards. Objective standards are those which are determined by the planned objectives of the business and can change as the objective changes as, for example, the sales target fixed for a sales representative through the sales budget. Operating standards have a degree of permanency and may remain unchanged for years until methods change, whereas objective standards may change annually or more frequently in accordance with the budget plan.

A foreman in a production department has to operate against both standards: he has to obtain the required output from each operator as determined by the operational times, and he has to obtain the total output projected by the production budget, or programme, in accordance with the number of productive operators budgeted to achieve it.

The higher levels of management generally operate against objective standards expressed in financial terms of income, costs and profit. Operating standards generally operate at the lower level of management in conjunction with the appropriate objective standards and, while costs are still important, performance is usually expressed in the more concrete terms of quantity and time.

Procedures and standards of performance have an important role in the efficiency of an organization and as more attention is devoted to them the operating results of the business will improve.

organization charts

There are several advantages in showing an organization in chart form. In the first place it gives management a clearer indication of the organization. It can be used to show each employee where he fits into the organization; not directly because workers do not appear on the chart, but by showing the position of his department within the organization structure. The companies who adopt this procedure are rewarded by the interest shown by employees and this can be a further step towards closer co-operation between management and worker.

There is the further consideration that it is often difficult to see the shape of the organization without seeing it in chart form. Anyone who has been called upon to examine organizations and make recommendations for their improvement will appreciate that only by charting the existing organization can one be sure of exposing the weaknesses. Furthermore if a chart of the existing organization is placed alongside a chart of the proposed organization then improvements can be readily apparent. Appendix 4 is an example of a typical organization chart for a medium-sized company.

the plan of organization

Products, markets and volume of sales are the significant factors that have to be taken into account in planning the organization. The product determines the technological requirements which in turn decide the qualifications of the design department, the production engineering department and other departments. The volume of sales can influence the organization because of the different techniques that apply as between large-scale operation and small-scale operation. The products and the markets decide the type of marketing organization required. If a business decides to extend into other product lines it must first provide the organization appropriate to these products.

The organization should be determined by what the products demand and not by what the business can afford to spend. If product sales are below the economic level necessary to support the right organization it can be an indication that the business is making the wrong products.

Authority to make decisions should be delegated to the lowest possible level and close to the facts. The authority should be decided by the status of the job and not by the ability of the person. Personnel should be trained to carry this responsibility. Delegation implies control and should preferably only be done when standards are fixed and when there is a regular flow of information to evaluate performance.

Standards, operating and objective, and procedures are essential to the success of any organization. Finally it is management itself which should have the greatest influence on the efficiency of the organization by giving it purpose, direction and co-ordination.

3 the production function

The economic function of the industrial enterprise is to supply a product that will satisfy market demand and sell at a profit. It is the production function that satisfies this demand by producing the product in the required quantity, of the right quality, at the required time and at a competitive cost. The production function translates the total efforts, skills and resources of a business into the tangible form that produces the sales income and the profit.

The other major functions are a means to this end. The marketing function through its contribution to the product policy ensures that the skills and resources of the business are applied to the best advantage. It establishes that there is a market demand for the product; it submits a product specification setting out the requirements of the market; it ensures a large enough share of the market to provide the volume necessary to enable the products to be made at a competitive cost. The product design function ensures that the product is in the form most acceptable to the market and is economical to produce. The financial control function harnesses the resources of the business and prevents erosion. But however well these functions perform they are dependent upon the production output for the fulfilment of their objectives.

the production function

The production function generally consists of four major sub-functions: the technical function, the production planning and control function, the manufacturing function and the plant maintenance function.

THE TECHNICAL FUNCTION This is often termed production engineering and it deals with the technical aspects of production which normally include the layout of the factory, the design or selection and location of plant and machinery, the design of tools, jigs and fixtures, planning the methods of production and work study. The methods of production may be built-in when designing the plant, as is quite often the case in process or flow production, and is tantamount to this in continuous production where the machines are permanently set-up to perform a single operation, or series of operations, on one part. In the manufacture of the assembly type of product in batch production, or jobbing, the methods of production are set out in an operations layout form for each part, sub-assembly and final assembly. The operations layout shows in respect of each part the materials specification and the quantity required, a description of each operation to be performed, the machine and the tools to be used for each operation and the allowed time for setting and operating. In the case of assembly it lists the parts to be assembled, the operations to be performed and the allowed time for each operation.

There is probably no function in a business which can be more rewarding, or more frustrating, than the technical function. It has to weigh up the pros and cons of the situation and not necessarily decide the best method of production and the facilities appropriate to it, but 'the best method in the circumstances'. It is a problem of matching the method and the production facilities to the economics of the situation, and this can be largely a question of the volume of production. A company manufacturing a product in various sizes decided to review its production methods in the light of recent developments in production machines. The major part called for ten operations on six different types of machines. It was ascertained that certain sizes sold in sufficient quantities to justify transfer machines and these were duly installed. Each transfer machine performed all the ten operations on two sizes. The sizes that did not justify transfer machines had to be produced less efficiently but more economically by present methods.

Volume is a significant factor in production efficiency and a business cannot be competitive when it has to sacrifice efficiency for economy, unless its competitors are similarly placed.

THE PRODUCTION PLANNING AND CONTROL FUNCTION
This function is concerned with obtaining the output required in terms of quantity and time. The technical function has decided 'how' the products will be produced and has provided the production facilities necessary to produce them within the limits generally classified as the production capacity. The production planning function has to make the maximum use of the production capacity insofar as the order book, or the production programme, will permit. Its objectives are the 'what' and 'when' of production.

Some confusion arises in practice through the term 'production planning'. It may sometimes be regarded as a technical function in the belief that it refers to the planning of the methods of production. The planning of output places it in a separate category and is the meaning given to it here.

The production planning and control function can be relatively simple or highly complex according to the type of product, the volume of production and the method of manufacture. In process or mass production it can be comparatively simple, but in batch production and some forms of jobbing work it can be complex. This function is usually responsible for the planning of production programmes in accordance with the order book, or instructions given, the scheduling of procurement and production, the issue of production orders and other production forms, determining delivery dates and controlling actual performance against schedule.

THE MANUFACTURING FUNCTION This is the hub of the business: the operating centre that produces the products. From the technical information available, either incorporated in the plant or contained in an operation layout, and from the production orders issued by production planning, the manufacturing function produces the products in the quality and quantity required.

THE MAINTENANCE FUNCTION The increase in mechanisation and automation, and the consequently larger investment in plant, are making more exacting demands on the maintenance function. Breakdowns are altogether too expensive to be acceptable and the maintenance function has to plan around preventive maintenance backed by inspection routines and detailed records. Planning and procedures are now important features in a function that is facing increasing responsibilities.

the types of production

No two companies are identical in their organization of production but certain types of product tend to be associated with certain types of production. The two factors that have the greatest influence on the type of production are the product and the volume of sales.

The generally recognised types of production are process, continuous, batch and jobbing. Process, or flow production, is the most advanced method and is usually fully automated. The plant is specially designed for the product and cannot generally be adapted for another product. The raw materials are fed in at one end, moved automatically between one production stage and another, and emerge as a finished product. Recording charts are usually inserted at strategic points in the plant to measure the flow. This type of manufacture is generally limited in its application to a homogeneous product, for example, chemicals, beer and oil refining.

Continuous production, sometimes termed mass production, usually applies to the assembly type of product manufactured in large quantities. The production of motor cars is the outstanding example. It attempts to simulate process production but falls short of it on account of the product. It is not fully automated in terms of the product but only for certain parts and processes. The characteristic of this type of production is that the machines are permanently set up to do a particular operation, or series of operations, thus avoiding delays through tool changes and queuing. It operates on the flow principle and stores are not usually provided. The co-ordination of the quantity produced at each production point is not automatic but has to be controlled to ensure a balanced flow of parts to the assembly lines.

Batch production can be generally regarded as a compromise between continuous production and jobbing. The volume is not sufficient to justify the large investment in plant necessary for continuous production but is generally greater than that provided by jobbing production. Batch production involves tool changes, queuing, control of quantities produced at the different operations and the provision of stores for accumulating and marshalling parts prior to assembly. The aim in batch production is to make the batch quantity as large as possible within the limits of an economic inventory.

Jobbing production operates when an article is made in small quantities to the specification of the customer. The manufacture of a prototype is a typical example. The jobbing manufacturer is generally equipped to make this class of products economically and he tends to use general-purpose machines which will involve the minimum set-up time since only small quantities are being produced.

In general, batch production presents the greatest difficulties and problems.

the production system

Every business has to develop the system that will best suit its product and its circumstances, and the one thing that is certain is that the ideal system never emerges; it has to be actively planned and implemented.

A review of the various types of production suggests that batch production provides the greatest potential for increasing productivity. Process and continuous production are already advanced systems operated by efficient companies and improvements are more likely to be achieved through increasing automation rather than improving systems. Jobbing is so restricted by the product considerations that marked improvements are unlikely. It is batch production that provides the scope for increasing productivity through improved systems and concepts and this will be considered in detail in a subsequent section.

the production organization

Production is a practical function and the plan of the production organization must be specific in its objectives. It must visualize the production system and the skills and duties it entails, and the demands that it will make on each activity. The type of production will determine the relative emphasis and importance to be attached to each section of the organization. In process production, for example, planning and control is generally simple and straightforward; in batch production it can be a complex and important operation. In continuous production the technical considerations can be exceedingly complex.

It is important to recognize the subsidiary functions contained in the total production function as the qualities required for each are distinctly different. The technical function requires trained engineers with ideas and a keen appreciation of the economics of production. The production planning function requires administrative and organizing ability. It is not, as some firms appear to regard it, a clerical function dealing with paperwork. The production function requires production knowledge and the ability to direct and supervise a number of people.

Planning an organization for batch production usually presents the most problems as is evidenced by the number of firms which never fully resolve them. In practice the organization of production itself is usually clearly defined; the departments with their foremen are shown together with their lines of responsibility. The main differences in the organization structure usually arise in connection with the technical function and the production planning function. There are companies that combine these two functions under the one head, who may be termed the production engineer or planning engineer. In the smaller companies this combination is understandable but generally this type of organization stems from the failure to appreciate the service that each performs and the different skills required.

Some companies are less efficient than they need be because of the weakness of the planning function: a condition that may well arise because management does not appreciate the importance of the function and, therefore, fails to create the right organization.

The production organization chart in Appendix 5 applies to an engineering company employing about 500 people and batch producing standard products.

It makes a clear distinction between the technical and the production planning functions in the belief, based on the experience of a number of companies, that an appreciation of the distinctive contribution each can make is an important factor in planning the right organization. The buyer and the personnel manager have been shown on the chart as reporting to the works manager but practice varies with regard to these functions.

batch production

The greatest scope for batch production probably lies with the business that makes standard products, or standard parts for products which vary only to a limited degree.

The first consideration is simplification and standardization in the design and manufacture of the products. Value engineering and value analysis have produced remarkable results in the simplification of products but their scope has not generally been extended to the standardization of parts. In this field the acceptance of a concept rather than particular abilities can be the decisive factor. This can be illustrated by the different outlook of two companies making the same product. One was a large company with 90 per cent of its output standardized. It made product A as a side line and orders were generally for one off to the particular requirements of the customer. The chief designer of the company described product A as 'a standard product with modifications' and he demonstrated this by showing that most of the parts were made in batches for stock. The other company made product A only and described it as 'a special product with a few common parts'. Comparatively few parts were manufactured in batches.

There are certain conditions which are generally inherent in batch production and these, together with their implications, are considered below.

production capacity

Production capacity insofar as it is represented by production machines is only in balance when the conditions are static. The business that makes a single product consisting of a number of parts will find that the balance changes as the demand for the product increases. The business that makes several products will never be in balance as any change in the mix or the volume will alter the position.

Many firms aim at establishing the work load on every machine at all times. More often than not this does not give an accurate picture, and it is not unusual to find that better results can be obtained simpler and cheaper through 'establishing the exceptions'. A study of the production capacity will show which class of machines tend to create 'bottlenecks'. Where there is difficulty in establishing this an efficient foreman can generally give good indications. Once the 'bottlenecks' have been established work load figures are maintained for them as these decide at any time the production capacity of the plant.

queuing and machine-setting

These are inevitable in batch production which, unlike continuous production, cannot economically justify the large investment in plant necessary to have machines permanently set-up to do a single operation, or series of operations. Queuing times cannot generally be established as conditions vary too much to make this possible. Therefore, while information can be provided through work measurement to show the time required to set up the machine and perform the operation there is generally little indication of the waiting time between operations. Many companies make an arbitrary allowance for queuing time by allowing one week for each operation, providing the production time does not exceed a week. The economics of batch production requires the batch quantity to be as large as possible without creating an excess inventory. Queuing makes the progressing of jobs essential and the progress section of the production planning department is an important factor in achieving the output target.

inventory control

There is probably no system so universal in its application or so widely used as the control, on a maximum/minimum basis, of stock quantities, or, as it is sometimes operated, on a re-order point and re-order quantity. The quantities are established on the basis of rate of usage, lead time, plus a safety factor, and the economic order quantity. It is a simple system to apply and there are few companies that cannot find a suitable application for it. Indeed this system has operated so well in some companies over an extended period that they have tended to confuse the system with the objective.

Continuous production presents a very good example of sophisticated inventory control. In this type of production the volume can be so large that millions of pounds are tied up in inventories and for this reason materials must always be moving to avoid the formation of costly 'reservoirs'. Storage facilities are not provided, and there is a constant endeavour to reduce the production, or throughput, time to minimize inventories.

Batch manufacturing, particularly in its application to the assembly type of product, has to operate in very different conditions and has generally to provide stores as a grouping, or marshalling point, for the accumulation of parts prior to assembly. But some companies have been slow to realize that although they cannot apply the principles of continuous production in total they may be able to apply them in part. An investigation will generally show, except perhaps for the smaller business, that some parts, probably the most expensive, can be economically obtained as required from suppliers. The normal procedure is to place a bulk order and to call off the quantities as required over an extended period in accordance with an agreed delivery schedule. This procedure can reduce inventories substantially as compared with the system of maximum/minimum stock replacement.

In batch production the two key factors from the viewpoint of inventory control are procuring purchased items against delivery schedules and establishing the minimum throughput time for the production of major parts. Obviously there will be limitations in how far these can be economically applied. The majority of the items, purchased or manufactured, will probably have to be ordered on a maximum/minimum stock replacement basis, but in value these may well be less than 50 per cent of the inventory. This procedure resolves itself into a question of distinguishing the important from the relatively unimportant and ensuring that the principles of continuous production are applied to major parts wherever these are economically practicable.

the production concept

Every firm has its peculiarities in its product range, its policies and methods, and in its organization, and it must strive for the systems that will best suit its requirements. One of the essential approaches is to analyse the products and the production operations, and a useful device for this purpose is an explosion chart which breaks the product down into major assemblies, sub-assemblies and parts, and in the case of manufactured parts shows the operations to be performed against a time scale. Appendix 6 illustrates the principles involved. From this analysis, in conjunction with cost figures, the major parts are segregated from the subsidiary and minor parts to see if any warrant special treatment. There are generally two methods that can be adopted in batch production: (*a*) the general method o placing an order for a given quantity when the re-order point is reached, or (*b*) preparing a production programme and scheduling deliveries and production in accordance with the programme. Method (*b*) is applicable to continuous production and cannot be fully applied to batch production where a compromise is necessary by preparing a production programme for the major parts and using method (*a*) for all other parts. Batch production becomes progressively efficient the more it simulates continuous production and this must be the objective.

The ideal method of producing the major parts is through line production wherever the investment in the necessary machines can be economically justified. The advantages are that the production cycle time of the parts, and therefore of the product, can be substantially reduced, assembly programmes and delivery dates are generally more reliable, and investment in inventories is lower.

Where the line production of major parts is not feasible, priority is given to their manufacture on all machines and the various operations are scheduled to close time limits. The manufacture of the other parts will be done on a stock replacement basis against pre-arranged order points and order quantities. In general these minor parts will have a generous maximum stock level as their value will be generally small, and they will be produced as the capacity is available with the minimum planning.

The policy with major parts, line produced or otherwise, is to feed them direct to assembly while ensuring that the other matching parts will be available in the finished parts store. The improvements made by the introduction of line production can be remarkable; in one case the throughput time of the product was reduced from fourteen weeks to three weeks, and in another case from six weeks to two weeks. It is true that line production involves an additional investment in machinery but the resulting decrease in inventories is an offsetting factor.

the production budget

An industrial organization cannot escape the obligation of planning ahead and committing itself to a course of action. The important difference between companies is that some have accepted and developed a planning discipline while others plan on the basis of improvisation and expediency. The size of a factory is the outcome of planning ahead. Many factories have reached their present size through growth. The company with a planning discipline may have anticipated the increased demand and prepared for it. The company that plans through expediency will generally wait until the demand is established before enlarging its capacity, probably losing valuable orders in the interim period. But even in this case anticipation is the important factor since the company must presume that the increased demand will be maintained. To maintain the demand a business must be in a position to take appropriate action and this can only be determined by forward planning based on a factual appraisal of the conditions. There must always be an element of uncertainty in forward planning but the truth is that a business will always operate more effectively and more profitably with it than without it.

The implications of long and short term production planning are

P.P.C.—4

mentioned in a subsequent section; the consideration at this point is the short term budget for actioning actual production.

Short term business planning usually operates within the framework of an annual budget and here the primary object is to agree sales and profit targets. A production budget has to be projected against the sales budget as a means of determining costs to arrive at profit targets. The annual budget constitutes a sales programme against which the achievements of the marketing department will be measured. Many companies will not commit themselves, however, to a production programme based on an annual budget. The production need is generally for short term forecasts for periods of up to six months which will keep the inventories at a reasonable level and prevent fluctuations in demand from upsetting a regular volume of production.

Many business concerns have to anticipate demand in the manufacture of parts or products and a reliable forecast is important. In general the period to be covered by the forecast cannot be less than the lead time for the products.

Forecasts can be based on:

1 Intuition backed by knowledge, experience, and judgement.
2 Mathematical analysis using a model based on previous demand.
3 A combination of 1 and 2.

It can generally be accepted that a combination will provide a more reliable forecast.

determining delivery promises

Where a standard product is produced and production is ahead of the order book then deliveries can be made from stock. Some companies make a point of delivering the product from stock. There are other companies which can deliver from stock on certain occasions or at particular periods of the year until the order book is in advance of production when a delivery date has to be quoted. In the case of jobbing work, and the standard product with modifications, orders are accepted against a quoted delivery date.

There are many companies that have to give a future delivery against orders and it is important both from the viewpoint of the customer and the supplier that there is a reliable basis for determining delivery dates. The general principle is to relate the orders outstanding for each product to the production programme for the product. If, for example, the order book shows orders totalling 10,000 and the production programme for the product is 1,000 per week then the delivery period for new orders cannot be less than eleven weeks. This can be an oversimplification of the procedure in some cases, particularly where it is the assembly type of product manufactured in batches. In this type of production the delivery date is generally determined by the capacity of the assembly department and the current work load as represented by the order book. The procedure operated by one company will illustrate the point. The company manufactured several products on batch production, one being meters of various sizes for metering liquids. There was one line for the assembly of all but the largest meters and the procedure was to issue a four-weekly programme, subdivided by weeks, a fortnight before the start of the period. But the production control department built up the work load on assembly as each order was received. If, for example, there was a full work load for eight weeks ahead then the next order received would be booked into the ninth week and the customer advised of the delivery date. In booking the order into the next available week the standard hours required to assemble the particular type of meter were recorded and when the total hours booked into the week reached the capacity of the assembly department subsequent orders were carried into the following week and the procedure repeated. In operating this procedure the company recognised three major parts and special care was taken to ensure that supplies were carefully scheduled to meet the assembly programme. The other parts, on a short production cycle, were not scheduled but the progress department had to ensure that supplies would be available for assembly.

These systems have proved their efficiency in practice, resulting in reliable deliveries and fostering good relations with customers.

planning production and controlling output

In every business the planning of output is of paramount importance both in the long and the short term. In the longer term the production capacity of the plant has to be related to the product policy and to the potential increase in market demand. This is a necessary precaution to ensure that the business at least maintains its share of the market. In the shorter term the business has to plan its output to make full use of its organisation and production facilities, and to ensure a reliable service to customers. It is also the medium for preserving the right balance between income and operating expenses.

Planning has to be a co-ordinated operation. It has to give the total view. Long and short term plans should operate within a common framework, the difference being the point of time at which action should be taken. Long term planning will usually cover a period of two to five years or more. It will have regard to the product policy, to new or improved product designs, to innovations in production methods, to market demand actual and potential, to share of the market actual and potential, and to the practicability of substitute or alternative products entering the market. The result of the long term plan, from the production viewpoint, will be to decide what increase in the production capacity is necessary and when it should be effective. This will be followed by a detailed scheme to be submitted for approval.

In some forms of flow production, and in continuous production, an increase in the production capacity can involve a large capital expenditure. In batch production and jobbing work the production capacity can usually be increased by stages thus limiting, or regulating, the capital expenditure undertaken at any one time.

The short term plan may be the annual budget with, or without, a shorter term budget. The type of production, the scale of operation, and the reliability of the sales forecast, can all influence the length of the period covered by a production programme. In continuous manufacture a year is a normal period for programming production, whereas in batch production there is a strong tendency to limit commitments to a shorter period.

The important factor in the efficient operation of a business is to maintain the level of output. The proportion of the total operating cost represented by fixed expenses is now so large that a comparatively small reduction in output can make the difference between a profit and a loss. The problem that can face most companies is how far to accumulate stocks of finished products against the run of the order book before reducing output. If a company acts too soon and directly or indirectly depletes a trained and experienced labour force it may take months to restore the output to its previous level and the profits will be adversely affected. Companies manufacturing seasonal products can be particularly vulnerable. To keep the plant to an economical size they may maintain production at a constant level throughout the year and consequently accumulate large stocks during the off-peak period. If the sales during the peak period are not up to expectations then they are left with large stocks or, conversely, if the sales exceed the planned output valuable business is lost.

The most critical planning problems normally lie within the production area because these plans commit the business to actual expenditure in anticipation of certain events: (a) the expenditure involved in increasing the capacity of the plant, and (b) purchasing commitments and production programming in advance of sales orders. It is virtually impossible for a business to perform these tasks effectively without competent planning backed by reliable forecasts and a marketing organization with the ability to influence sales.

The last stage in production planning is the production programme which states the number of units to be produced, determines the delivery requirements from suppliers, and fixes the manufacturing schedule. The control of output varies with the type of production. In process and continuous production where all operations are virtually co-ordinated from start to finish and generally compressed into a short period cycle, the control of output is simply a matter of comparing the quantity made with the programme. In batch production of the assembly product, and in certain types of jobbing work, the quantity is again an indication of production performance, but not completely as all operations are not co-ordinated as with flow and continuous production, and there is no measure of the fluctuation of work-in-progress and the work content represented by it. A good performance in the number of products made could, if it were known, be marred by a sharp decline in work-in-progress. A supplementary control, as mentioned later, can usefully bridge this gap.

In the assembly type of product the planning of production is centred on the assembly line, and the distinguishing mark of the efficient business is the infinite pains taken in setting this up as advantageously as human ingenuity will permit. Mass production as first introduced by Henry Ford was only made possible by the moving assembly line. The assembly line sets the capacity and the pace of production. Once the assembly programme is fixed parts and sub-assemblies have to be fed to the final assembly line in the required quantity at the required time. Many companies could improve their productivity and over-all efficiency by a close study of their assembly operations. Many methods engineering departments consider their work only extends to the manufacture of parts, and quite often the drawing office will dictate the grouping of parts into sub-assemblies and final assembly which, as is only to be expected, is not logical from a production viewpoint.

measuring productivity

This can be a frustrating problem in many companies unless, as previously mentioned, they are engaged in process or continuous production. It is important to recognise that in all types of production the number of units produced against the programme is a significant and valid measure of performance. It provides the basis, for example, for short term profit budgeting which is in itself an important factor. Its limitation lies in the fact that while it is a measure of performance it is not in every case a measure of productivity.

The only means available to many companies of measuring productivity is through work measurement which is the time factor of an operation as determined by work study. It is customary to express the time factor in terms of a 'standard hour' which is a definite unit of work and is the time an operator should take when operating at a '60' performance. At this level of performance, which represents the speed of an operator working without an incentive, the time actually taken will be equal to the time allowed. In practice an operator is expected to operate above a '60' performance (normally not less than an '80') and the standard hours produced should therefore always exceed the actual hours taken.

The standard hours content of each product (analysed by departments), multiplied by the quantity of each product to be produced in a given period, sets the production target. This is translated into the number of standard hours to be produced each week by each department.

The next point to be decided is the number of operators to be employed in each department to meet this programme and here the following factors have to be taken into account.

1 THE UTILIZATION FACTOR A productive operator will not be fully occupied on production during the whole of his attendance hours. He will certainly lose some time: perhaps waiting for his machine to be set up, or waiting for materials or job instructions. Again not all of the jobs he is engaged on will be productive; he may have to spend time on rectification work, cleaning his machine and other sundry jobs. This may well account for 5 to $7\frac{1}{2}$ per cent of his attendance hours.

2 PERFORMANCE The level of performance required from the average operator while working on production jobs will have to be determined—probably not less than an '80' performance.

If, therefore, a particular department is programmed to produce 1,200 standard hours per week the number of operators required is calculated as follows:

Standard hours per week = 1,200

Equivalent actual hours at '80' performance $\frac{60}{80}$ = 900

Allow for non-utilization: 5 per cent = 947 hr

$\frac{(900 \times 100)}{95}$

Number of operators at 40 hr/week = 24

The above information is then recorded on a weekly operating statement for the foreman of the department and works management as shown in Appendix 7. A similar statement is prepared for each department, with a summary of all departments. The programme is listed on the first line of the statement and the actual figures are shown week by week for the duration of the programme. The control statement is changed as the programme changes.

summary

The production function must be an important factor in every industrial concern as it is the volume of saleable output that determines the income of the business. It is the responsibility of top management to ensure that the organization and the concepts and practices of the production function are geared to the particular requirements of the business. It is also the responsibility of management to ensure that the production function is given the opportunity to operate economically, that is on the same terms at least as those of competitors. If the volume of sales imposes economic restrictions on the means and methods of production this could be a competitive weakness. Whatever the short term requirements may be, there is no future for a business in marginal production.

The aim of production is to remove the present limiting factors by extending the frontiers of knowledge. The manufacture of a homogeneous product in quantity has led to process production which is probably the most advanced form. Continuous, or mass production, was developed for the manufacture of large quantities of an assembly product. These results have been achieved by applying logic to an objective and developing new concepts. The moving assembly line was an example of a new concept that had a tremendous impact in the production field. Now the aim is to extend the application of automation.

The companies presently engaged in process and mass production are intent on extending the application of automation, and developing new and improved methods of manufacturing. These are the pioneers of new production concepts. For the majority of companies, and 90 per cent of the total employ less than 500 persons, the task is how to condition themselves to be able to apply, in part at least, the concepts and practices common to the most advanced types of production.

A large cross-section of industry is engaged in batch production in one form or another. Some of the products are comparatively simple and present no particular production problem. Others can be quite complex and the assembly type of product consisting of a large number of parts is probably the most complicated of all forms of production. It is in this field that opportunities lie for the application of more advanced production methods.

The first consideration is to recognise that 'to attempt too much is to achieve little'. The product must first be analysed into the important and the relatively unimportant parts on the basis of cost of each and the time required to produce. In an average analysis not more than 10 per cent of the parts will rank as important enough to be singled out for special consideration and treatment. The aim will be to deal with these special parts as in continuous production, that is to schedule deliveries of materials to arrive close to the time required and to have line production on machines reserved for the purpose. In many cases the machines may be adaptable to handle several sizes of the same part. In one company the body casting was the most important part of the product and a line of six machines was installed to perform all the operations on the three sizes of body. After several years' production was further advanced by installing one transfer machine which performed all the operations and displaced the six existing machines.

Where the line production of any major part cannot economically justify the investment in plant then the alternative procedure is adopted. The alternative is to plan the manufacture of the major parts against a strict time schedule, giving them priority in the work load of all the machines used for their production. This procedure establishes reliable dates for the completion of the major parts and the progress function has to ensure that the matching minor parts will be available at the same time for assembly. The supplies of minor parts are generally obtained through predetermined order points and order levels. In some firms the production of minor parts is not planned other than to ensure that there is available capacity for their manufacture.

These comparatively simple procedures can definitely improve output and provide a better delivery service to customers. When a company tries to schedule the production of every part, major and minor, and include it in the work load of each machine, or group of similar machines, there is generally more confusion than order as a result, and if there is any fundamental weakness, such as a bottleneck on a particular group of machines, it seldom exposes the weakness. This is hard to believe but practice shows it to be generally the case.

4 management accounting

Management accounting owes its present leading position to several factors but probably two of the main reasons are that it operates in a medium which is of supreme importance to management—income, expenditure and profit—and can present facts of great diversity on a common basis as quite often financial terms are generally the only means of expressing and relating a number of variables.

Management accounting operates in three time dimensions: in the past in providing historical profit statements; in the present in controlling operating efficiency; in the future through planned objectives and budgetary control.

The principal role of management accounting should be to develop financial statements and cost information for management decisions. Its other functions can be summarised briefly as:

1 Providing period profit statements and balance sheets.
2 Aiding management in developing product policies and selling price structures.
3 Aiding management in developing business objectives through long and short term plans.
4 Providing comparative statements for measuring operating efficiency.

In brief, management accounting is indispensable to management in getting to know and understand the business and in determining its future prospects.

The function of management accounting is to 'translate' information and facts into figures. For the most part it is concerned with 'comparisons' and the preparation of financial statements and cost information that show the results achieved against the standards set. The policies, attitudes and actions of management largely condition the effectiveness of the management accounting function and its standard of performance. Dynamic management dedicated to the efficient operation of a business and using every tool at its disposal to this end will create the right conditions to obtain the maximum benefits from management accounting. It will ensure that standards of performance are set wherever practicable and that objectives are factually planned and clearly defined, and it is only within this framework that management accounting can function effectively.

There are generally two standards that operate within a business: the performance standard and the operational standard; and together these normally provide a total measure of the performance of a business. In an engineering business performance standards would normally be set for the time required to perform a particular operation, the quantity of material to be used to produce a given number of parts and a standard allowance for rejects. Performance standards are usually of fairly long duration and only change when the method of production changes or the product is redesigned. Operational standards, on the contrary, are usually of short duration. These are normally determined by period budgets and are changed, or reviewed, at the end of each budget period. The number of productive operators to be employed to obtain the budgeted output, or indeed the number of people to be employed in any department to achieve the planned objective, are typical examples of operational standards.

Management accounting has its own inherent problems, e.g. relating expenses with varying characteristics to output and sales.

It has to be emphasised that management accounting does not determine performance or operational standards; this is the function and responsibility of management. Without these standards a business is confined to historical accounting with strictly limited advantages since there are no yardsticks to pinpoint good or bad performance. This is not only a negative approach to management accounting but it constitutes a negative approach to the management of a business.

expense control

Expenses are segregated to give a fair indication of what they comprise; this is important to ensure that the amount incurred under each expense heading can be identified and properly controlled. It is not enough, for example, to group all the wages paid under one heading; a subdivision will be necessary to show the wages paid to productive operators, to indirect workers, to inspectors, etc., as determined by the requirements of the business. The next stage is to charge the expense to the department or cost centre which incurred it. Some expenses are not incurred directly by a specific department but are spread over a number of departments and common expenses which have to be shared are known as 'allocated' expenses. In controlling the expenditure of each department it is the general practice to regard the head of the department as responsible for direct expenses but not for allocated expenses which are the responsibility of a higher management level.

From the viewpoint of the control of expenditure it is customary to allocate responsibility in accordance with the responsibilities prescribed by the organisation structure. In general there are four main divisions in the average manufacturing business: research and development and product design, marketing, production and finance; and the executive in charge will be responsible for the expenditure incurred by his division. The executive will, in turn, allocate responsibilities to his subordinates. The following illustration shows the application of this principle in the production division.

PRODUCTION DIRECTOR

Production	Production Manager	Responsible for:
		1 All production departments
		2 Maintenance Department
		3 Tool Department
		4 Internal Transport

SERVICES DEPARTMENTS

Methods Engineering	Production Engineer	1 Methods Engineering 2 Work Study 3 Tool Design
Production Planning	Production Controller	1 Planning and Scheduling 2 Progress Department 3 Stock Control 4 Stores Control
Purchasing	Buyer	Purchasing Department
Personnel Administration	Personnel Manager	Personnel Matters

This principle will be extended further; for example the production manager will hold each foreman responsible for his particular department and the direct expenditure incurred.

Some companies operate in the manner indicated but impose certain variations. Here are two illustrations:

1 Inspectors operating in production departments were functionally responsible to the Chief Designer for directions and instructions through the Quality Controller but responsible to the Production Manager for discipline. It was ruled that the cost of this inspection was a legitimate charge to production since it could influence the cost through quality of workmanship.
2 Depreciation of plant and machinery was not charged to the production departments but to the chief executive since it was considered to be a policy decision. Other companies charge this to the departments concerned as they consider this the only means of arriving at the true loss arising from the failure of a department to meet its production target.

The expenses to be incurred by each department or section are fixed by expense budgets but there is a real difficulty about the control of expenditure in that it does not vary in accordance with output. There is often the further complication in many companies that there is no real yardstick for measuring output. In many manufacturing concerns the only directly variable expense is production materials.

Productive labour which is normally regarded as a directly variable expense may require a 10 per cent (sometimes 20 per cent) variation in output before it is affected, other than to eliminate overtime working if any.

In the average business a reduction in output due to a trade recession of up to 20 per cent may not produce a reduction in expenditure of more than 2 to 3 per cent if production materials are excluded. Company policy is a factor and the desire to maintain an organization intact during what may be regarded as a short term recession tends to keep expenditure fixed. In general, expenses tend to be fixed in the short term where the decline in output does not exceed 10 to 15 per cent. In the long term, particularly where the variation in output is substantial, few expenses are fixed. A break-even chart is generally regarded as a useful medium for illustrating the cost-volume-profit relationship of a business and this will now be considered.

break-even chart

Figure 1 shows a typical break-even chart. The horizontal scale shows the capacity expressed as percentages; this is better expressed in physical units but this is seldom practicable. Several assumptions are made in drawing a break-even chart; firstly that the variable costs increase uniformly as the sales increase, and secondly that fixed expenses are constant throughout the full range of the capacity. These assumptions are not strictly true but generally suffice to give a pictorial representation.

The break-even point can be calculated independent of the chart by the following formula:

$$\frac{\text{Fixed expenses, £'s}}{\text{Selling price per unit} - \text{variable cost per unit}}$$

In a break-even chart where it is not possible to show units the formula has to be adjusted to show the break-even point related to volume of sales:

$$\frac{\text{Fixed expenses, £'s}}{\text{Sales £1} - \text{variable cost per £1 of sales}}$$

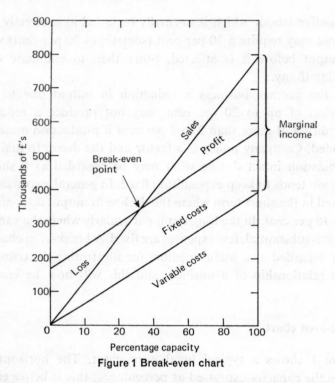

Figure 1 Break-even chart

If the fixed expenses for the period are £100,000 and the variable cost per £1 of sales is say £0.5 the calculation of the break-even is

$$\frac{\text{Fixed expenses £100,000}}{\text{Sales £1} - \text{variable expenses per £1 of sales £0·5}}$$

The break-even point is reached at £200,000 of sales. It is apparent also that beyond the break-even point the profit is £0.5 on every £1 of sales.

A break-even chart is indicative rather than accurate but it is useful as a graphical presentation of the structure of the business. In some cases it has inspired management to lower the break-even point.

It has its limitations inasmuch as no business is operated to break-even and in many companies a 10 per cent variation above or below the normal output level is the maximum swing that they are likely to experience and within this range expenditure, excluding production materials, tends to be relatively fixed.

Most companies operate above the break-even point or otherwise they would cease to exist. What is important to them is to establish the 'economic output level'. This can be a complex operation and before examining it in detail it is necessary to consider (a) how capacity is measured and (b) the sales contribution of a business and its profit strategy.

measuring capacity

The first point that has to be noted is that sales income does not measure capacity except in very rare and exceptional circumstances. The experience of one company operating in ideal conditions will illustrate the point. The company was engaged in the processing of one homogeneous product which was packaged in cartons of 112 pounds weight. The plant operated 24 hours per day throughout the year except for two stoppages of one week each for major overhauls. Throughout a period of two years the maximum output was obtained and sold. The product was sold in the home market and in most countries overseas but the selling price varied with the market. In each of the two years the quantity produced and sold varied by less than one-half per cent but the sales income varied by more than five per cent.

In process production where the plant produces only one homogeneous product the production capacity can be easily determined. In continuous production, for example the motor industry, the capacity of the assembly lines normally determines the capacity of the plant and there is generally no difficulty in establishing this. It is in batch production, particularly in the manufacture of engineering products, that the difficulties are encountered in measuring the production capacity where more than one product is produced. The difficulties are increased where there is no natural unit of output and a synthetic unit has to be adopted such as the standard hour.

P.P.C.—5

The standard hour is a very effective index for controlling performance and measuring productivity but it cannot be extensively used for
determining capacity, for example an hour on an expensive transfer
machine is a very different proposition from, say, an hour on a
drilling machine. It follows that a standard hour can only be used
effectively when it is weighted by certain factors. It also follows that
the number of factors used should be minimised as with each factor
introduced the variability potential is increased and this could
impair the consistency of the measurement.

Most factories have now reached the stage, or are progressing
towards it, where the machine is the key factor in production, certainly
from the cost viewpoint. Assembly departments are, perhaps, the
exceptions but even here the trend is towards mechanisation and in
some cases automation. The fact that the machine hour can be more
important than the man hour has to be recognised in considering
production capacity.

The factors selected for the weighting of the standard hour and the
procedure associated with them are dealt with in Appendix 8. The
information presented, being based on assessments, can never be
strictly accurate but it provides guidelines in the form of standards
that are not only useful as a measure of capacity but permit management to exercise effective control over performance at the very heart
of production. The costs associated with the selected factors can be
classed as the 'direct production costs'. In this group are contained
the expenses which have the closest relation to output in their move-
ment, with the exception of production materials; the obvious
example is direct, or productive, labour. Outside this area expenses
are less directly associated with output and vary to a smaller extent
with fluctuations in output.

sales contribution and profit strategy

The contribution made by the industrial business is the value added
in converting purchased materials into saleable products. The value

added can be simply determined by deducting the cost of the production materials from the selling price of the product. This added value, or sales contribution, should cover all the costs of operating the business and leave a profit margin. In short the total costs of a business fall into two distinctive categories: the materials content of the products and the cost of operating the business. It would be logical to assume that the profit contained in the selling price would have some relationship to the sales contribution but in practice it is difficult to establish any close connection between the selling price and cost of any product or even between the costs of the different manufacturers of the same products. These conditions reflect the complexities and vagaries of selling prices and costs.

The average business that manufactures several products may not be able to exert much influence on selling prices but it can formulate its profit strategy to obtain the maximum profit by establishing the most profitable product mix. The scope for concentrating on the most profitable product mix may, however, be fairly restricted in some companies dependent upon the marketability of the products and the flexibility of the production facilities. The art, or the science, of profit strategy is in no small measure dependent upon the ability to determine which are the more profitable products and this is not the simple process that some companies believe it to be.

A company selected from its product range the two products that it considered the most profitable. These were good selling lines and the objective was to increase the sales. The sales and cost figures are quoted below:

Method 1	Product A	Product B
	£	£
Selling price	120	100
Cost	90	80
Profit	30	20
Profit as percentage of cost	33⅓	25

There was no possible doubt that A was the more profitable product. As part of the general survey of profit strategy it was decided to examine the elements of the product cost for every product. This gave the following figures for A and B:

Method 2	Product A	Product B
	£	£
Selling price	120	100
less Materials cost	20	45
Contributed sales	100	55
less Operating cost	70	35
Profit	30	20
Profit as percentage of operating cost	43	57

In view of the apparent contradiction shown by the two methods it was decided that the proper basis was to relate the profit to the proportion of the production capacity absorbed by each product. It was not possible to ascertain the production capacity in the time available as the company used standard hours which were not weighted. It was agreed as a compromise to use the conversion cost as the basis and this gave the following figures:

Method 3	Product A	Product B
	£	£
Materials cost	20	45
Conversion cost	50	25
Selling, administration, etc.	20	10
Total cost	90	80
Selling price	120	100
Profit	30	20
Profit on conversion cost	60%	80%

It was finally decided that B, contrary to the original belief, was the more profitable product. In relating profit to conversion cost as the yardstick for measuring profitability another product was found which gave a better return than A. This product had never been pushed by the marketing department as it had only a minor part in the profit strategy but it proved to have a good sales potential.

The lesson learned by the company from this operation was that the ratio of profit to total cost can be completely misleading. Conditions may operate in some companies that make total cost a reliable basis, but for most companies the ratio of the profit to the capacity absorbed will probably be the only true index. The difficulty in establishing the P/C (profit/capacity) ratio is that few companies have the capacity information required.

profit planning and control

Some of the more important points that have to be considered in the planning and control of profits are:

What is the normal volume of output and the normal profit?

What is the volume of output that will produce an economic profit?

What is the planned volume of output and the profit target budgeted for the financial year?

What is the maximum volume variance above or below the planned volume that the business could experience?

What is the total production capacity of the plant?

The above considerations will not have the same significance for every business; much will depend on the efficiency of the particular company.

The normal volume and normal profit represent the average performance of a business over an extended period. If the business is efficient it will almost certainly be earning an economic profit. If the business is not earning an economic profit at this level of operation then the first task of management is to determine the action necessary to earn it. It may be necessary to sell more, or to concentrate on a more profitable product mix, or to eliminate products that are losing money, or to reduce costs. Management must determine the requirements and it is then a question of implementation insofar as the circumstances will permit. If basic considerations are involved, for example redesign because of the low market rating of existing products, or the need to introduce new products to offset shrinking markets for current products, then it will depend upon the resources of the business as to whether management can buy the time necessary to apply the appropriate remedies. The business that is marginal or close to it is in a difficult position as the profit earned is too low to create resources or to attract capital.

In planning the volume of output for the annual budget management must be aware of the normal output level and normal profit and how this compares with the volume required to earn an economic profit. An assessment of the influence of outside forces on trade prospects and the impact of competition direct and indirect will have to be considered in conjunction with internal decisions and actions taken to improve the efficiency and competitive power of the business. An annual budget is at best a factual assessment of what can be expected but with so many variables involved in the estimates there is always an element of uncertainty and because of this a company should consider the most that can be expected and the least, and project volume and profit figures for these maximum and minimum levels. This will then present management with the total field of sales and profit control for the financial year. The annual budget should enable the efficient company to strengthen its position and the marginal business to exploit the conditions to the maximum advantage; in every case effective planning will ensure that a business earns a better profit than it would do without it.

The maximum production capacity of the plant must be known to ensure that the output budgeted by the sales budget is attainable, and to indicate the cost to the business of excess capacity. It will be appreciated, of course, that the long term plan, of which the annual budget is a part, should have provided for any additional production capacity required to meet sales expansion.

The annual budget procedure incorporates the performance and operational standards required to compare actual results against the planned objectives.

Figures 2 and 3 show the procedure in chart form. Figure 2 shows the anticipated sales planned in the budget and the maximum and minimum sales figures. Against these are plotted the corresponding production material costs to show the sales contribution. Where a

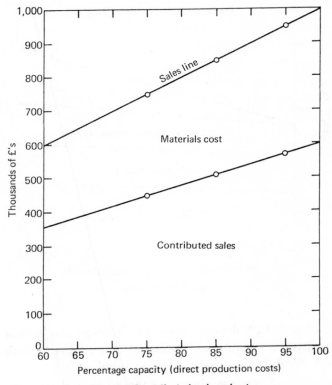

Figure 2 Contributed sales chart

business manufactures a variety of product, or several sizes of the same product, it usually follows that the ratio of the material content to total cost varies with every product and also the profit, and because of these two factors sales volume does not measure production volume. Materials cost is usually by far the larger variable and by eliminating this the variation brought about by a change in the product mix can be largely eliminated.

Figure 3 shows the sales contribution transferred from Figure 2. The costs are sub-divided into production costs, under the two

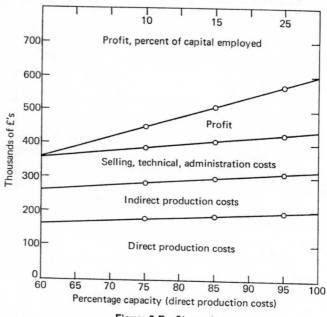

Figure 3 Profit graph

headings of 'direct production costs' and 'indirect production costs', and administration selling and technical costs. Obviously the costs can be sub-divided into greater detail as required.

The measure of capacity shown on the horizontal scale should be based on natural units of output or failing this, on the direct production costs, which should be the weighted standard hours, or on the total production costs. The horizontal scale at the top of the chart shows the ratio of profit to the capital employed. All points have been connected by a straight line for simplicity but this will not follow in practice.

standard costing

A standard cost is the cost attainable when operating at an acceptable standard of efficiency and at an economic level of output. Standard costs measure the efficiency of the operation of a business and provide product costs for comparison with selling prices.

The standards used in standard costing can be generally classified as (*a*) performance standards and (*b*) operational standards. In general terms performance standards can be described as the performance expected in doing particular jobs, and operational standards as the volume of operations and the expenditure appropriate to it. Performance standards are relatively permanent in their application and have little or no connection with operating standards, for example the time allowed to perform a particular operation or the quantity of parts or product that should be obtained from a given quantity of material. Performance standards only change as a rule with the redesign of the product or changes in the method of production. Performance standards, standards of procedure and departmental or shop practices, can make a significant contribution to the efficiency of a business and should be established wherever practicable.

Operational standards are related to volume and can only be determined when the operational level is decided, preferably through a budget representing the planned objective. Operational standards are subject to review and amendment every budget period. The operational volume as set by the sales budget determines the material costs, the direct and indirect production expenditure, and the other expenditure to be incurred by the business. The performance standards, plus the operational standards of volume and expenditure, usually provide most of the information necessary for management to direct and control the profitable operation of the business. It is the formulation of these standards that makes standard costing possible.

Performance standards are generally established for:

1 MATERIALS The type of materials and the quantity to be used in the manufacture of the product. This normally includes an

allowance for waste, or alternatively the standard yield to be obtained from a given quantity of material. In the assembly type of product this information is given for each manufactured part.

2 PRODUCTION TIME This is the standard time fixed for producing a product or a quantity of the product. In engineering products of the assembly type a standard time is fixed for each operation on each part and for the assembly of the product; also the department to perform each operation and the machine group to be used.

3 SPOILAGE ALLOWANCE This is the standard allowance for spoilage or rectification due to faulty workmanship.

4 STANDARD BATCH SIZES This is to ensure that the production facilities are used economically and that a proper relation is maintained between the preparation and setting time and the machine running time.

Operational standards usually comprise:

1 NUMBER OF PERSONS TO BE EMPLOYED In total and subdivided by departments. The different grades of labour will also be nominated. This 'head count' is very useful for the over-all control of the personnel employed.

2 SALARY AND WAGE RATES These are usually determined by the budget.

3 STANDARD PRICES The prices fixed by the purchasing department for each production material to be used.

4 STANDARD EXPENDITURE The amount to be incurred against each expense item and the charge or allocation to the departments concerned.

One of the important functions of standard costing is to measure the results achieved against the standards set and to establish variances by responsibilities. Variances involving standards of performance can generally be well defined but volume variances can be more complex in view of the incidence of fixed and partly variable expenses. Volume variances will be considered later when dealing with flexible budgets.

The application of standard costing can be simply illustrated by reference to a company processing a single homogeneous product. This is not a complex application but it clearly illustrates the principles involved in all standard costing systems regardless of the industry.

In this process raw materials are fed into the plant and conveyed automatically through a series of operations until they emerge as a finished product. The operation is continuous and the flow of materials is automatically recorded on a 24-hour chart. The yield obtained could vary with the materials used and the chemists make regular checks daily to record the yield.

The standard rate of output per hour was established from the capacity of the plant and the yield that could normally be expected from the standard quality of the materials used. These were the performance standards.

The next consideration was to establish the operational standards. It was planned that the plant would work for 24 hours per day through three eight-hourly shifts and this allowed an assessment to be made of the expenditure to be incurred. Standard materials prices were decided.

It was decided that the standard costs would be calculated on a standard four-weekly period as follows:

	£
Standard output for the period (tons)	
Materials cost (yield 90 per cent)	
Production costs:	
Wages	
Salaries	
Other expenses	
Total	
Standard cost per ton	
Standard cost per 112 pounds	5 : 12 : 0

Needless to say the cost sheet was actually prepared in much greater detail.

Every four weeks a statement of the actual output and expenditure was prepared and compared with standard. The over-all variances could be simply established by comparing the actual cost for 112 pounds with the standard cost. Variances were analysed in relation to output, yield, material price differences and expenditure.

the annual budget

Reference has been made previously to certain aspects of the annual budget; at this point the object is to summarise its purpose and objectives.

Sales and profit planning are long term considerations. To maintain and promote sales and profit a business must look closely at its products and its markets. If new models of current products have to be designed, or new products introduced, these are projects that can take two to five years or more to accomplish. If the aim is to establish new markets this is again a long term operation. If by virtue of these operations the production capacity has to be increased to accommodate an increase in sales this is also a long term project. These plans are outside the scope of an annual budget.

The annual budget is part of the long term budget—the final part. It is the function of the annual budget to translate the long term projects into sales and profit as they fall due for implementation.

The annual budget is for most companies a sales and profit budget. From the profit viewpoint a year is a suitable period for a business to take stock of its position; to assess the likely trading conditions, the state of the economy and the probable influence of government action, the effect of direct and indirect competition on its share of the market, the size of the total market and its growth potential, the probable effect of long term projects that are due for implementation and other internal actions designed to improve the operation of the business—these are some of the considerations that will permit a company to evaluate its sales and profit prospects.

A sales budget, once it is accepted by the board of directors, is more than a statement of expectations; it is a sales programme for the marketing division with quotas for all sales representatives and the performance is measured by the results obtained.

There are companies which make the sales budget the basis for a production programme and a full operational budget. The majority of companies, however, accept the sales budget as a standard of performance for the marketing division and develop production and other budgets from it, not with a view to immediate implementation but as a means of calculating the costs to be set against income to project the potential profit.

The criticism of the annual budget is that it projects costs against a fixed volume of output and if there is any variation from this fixed point the costs are no longer relevant due to the incidence of fixed and variable expenses. This would be true if the annual budget was planned as an operational budget but in most applications it is firstly a factual appraisal of the profit the business should earn and which it must endeavour to realize, and secondly an operational budget for the marketing division. In addition it is the basis frequently adopted for accounting and inventory valuation.

The operational budget for production is for most companies a short term budget varying usually from a period of one month up to six months. The period has to suit the individual requirements of a business and should generally coincide with the period of the production programme. It is a fixed budget for a scheduled volume of production.

It is important to appreciate the purpose and objectives of an annual budget; much of the criticism associated with it is due to a misunderstanding of its purpose and mistaking it for a total operational budget which in most cases it is not intended to be.

flexible budgets and short term budgets

A flexible budget is generally introduced to operate in conjunction with the annual budget. Unlike the annual budget which shows the expenditure related to a fixed volume of output the flexible budget shows the expenditure appropriate to various levels of output. If the volume changes the expenditure appropriate to it is known and this can then be compared with the actual expenditure as a means of control and allocating responsibility. A flexible budget is in effect an expense control budget and therefore performs a limited function as compared with an operational budget. It is usefully employed by companies but the alternative short term fixed budget applied to scheduled output gives greater control in that it controls performance as well as expenditure. Figure 4 shows the principle of flexible budgets with a few expenses taken as an example.

FLEXIBLE BUDGET: PRODUCTION COSTS

Period _____

Department _____
Cost centre _____

Expenses	Fixed Variable	Capacity, percent			
		70	80	90	100
		£	£	£	£
Direct labour	V	1,400	1,600	1,800	2,000
Indirect labour	V	800	840	880	920
Supervision	F	220	220	220	220
Supplies	V	240	250	260	270
Loose tools	V	200	215	230	245
Power and light	V	180	195	210	225
Repairs and maintenance	V	220	220	240	240
Depreciation plant	F	450	450	450	450
Establishment charges	F	120	120	120	120
Total		3,830	4,110	4,410	4,690

Figure 4 Flexible budget

The short term budget which is used in the planning and control of production and expenditure is a fixed budget with expenditure allocated against a definite volume of output as defined by the production programme or production schedule. In this short term budget the emphasis is on output and since operating expenses are relatively fixed any failure to obtain it represents a loss. This will be considered in detail in a later section.

product costs and selling prices

Products can be broadly classified as standard and non-standard from the viewpoint of selling price procedure; the business that manufactures standard products generally issues price lists whereas orders for non-standard products are normally placed against price quotations. In every case it is essential that a business should know its product costs.

A selling price reflects a number of factors which are generally summed up in what the market is prepared to pay. The market price may or may not be specific but it is usually relative and the supplier who demands a higher price for its product will have to justify it. One of the factors that influence price is product cost—not the cost of the individual manufacturer but of the industry as a whole. A product cost is not a simple fact; it is a summation of basic costs and volume costs as well as other factors. A product may have all the basic characteristics to compete successfully, that is be well designed to satisfy the standards of the market and economical to produce, but unless the business operates at or above the production volume level common throughout the industry the selling price will not be competitive.

A business should develop its product costs from its operating experience and the application of certain guiding principles. It should evaluate its product costs at a particular volume level which will produce an economic profit, that is a profit which will enable the business to operate effectively. Volume level is important because it pinpoints the fixed expenses that will be charged to the product. It is reported that for many years General Motors based its costing and price-fixing on 80 per cent of its production capacity although it regularly operated above this level. Obviously at an 80 per cent production level the company was earning a satisfactory profit. The assumption in fixing the volume of capacity is that it represents efficient operation and results in a fair price to the customer; if the business operates above this level it is entitled to higher profits for higher efficiency but if it operates below it the reduction in profits is a loss to the business. The difference in product costs with changes in volume reflects the incidence of fixed expenses.

A company manufacturing non-standard products increased its output every year for several years and its overheads, expressed as a rate per hour, steadily dropped. New overhead rates were calculated each year and used in the calculation of product costs and selling prices with the result that all the benefits of increased volume were passed on to the customer. When the significance of this procedure was made apparent the company adopted a production level of 80 per cent for product costing and price-fixing, an arrangement that proved satisfactory.

Most companies will be operating at a capacity level on average to earn a viable profit—not perhaps a satisfactory profit but at least an economic profit that will permit the business to maintain its competitive position. In these conditions it can be generally stated that a company is operating at normal capacity and normal efficiency and earning an economic profit and this constitutes the basis for product costing. The more efficient companies will be earning a surplus profit at their operating capacity and will, as previously shown, adopt a lower level of capacity for product costing and price-fixing. Conversely the business that is a marginal producer, or operating at a level not far removed from the break-even point, will have to project its product costs above its normal operating level to a point where an economic profit could be earned. Product costs have to be related to an economic production level actual or projected. The need to increase the volume to an economic production level for product costing purposes is not just an exercise on paper as management must provide ways and means of implementing it if the business is to survive.

The business that produces standard products will generally use its product costs as a measure of its ability to meet the market price rather than as a means of fixing the selling price. The manufacturer of non-standard products will have to be guided by its costs in submitting price quotations but here there is scope for flexibility and discretion in fixing the price according to the state of the order book. In every case product costs based on an operating level that will produce an economic profit are the essential conditions for price-fixing or price comparisons.

marginal costs

No company should be in business to earn marginal profits or to regularly produce a product that only earns a marginal profit. There can be occasions, however, when a business may find it expedient and profitable to sell a product in a marginal price market, or to introduce a product with a marginal profit, as a temporary measure to utilize surplus capacity. The emphasis should be on temporary as a business should plan to utilise its surplus capacity to earn a normal profit.

The idea behind marginal costing is that the fixed expenses have to be met by the current volume of output and if the output can be increased the only additional charge incurred is the variable or 'out-of-pocket' expenses. If the additional output can be sold at a price that covers the variable expenses plus a contribution to fixed expenses then the total profits of the business will be increased.

Marginal costing usually applies in two conditions: selling the product in a marginal price market, or manufacturing an additional product. In the first case an estimate is made of the increase in volume that would result from the acceptance of marginal selling prices and product costs are then projected against this higher output level. The practice of several companies is to take the normal factory cost of the product and add the normal profit and this is then expressed as a price discount which gives the minimum price to be quoted or accepted. At the lowest selling price there is no contribution for marketing and administration expenses.

P.P.C.—6

In the case of an additional product, the 'out-of-pocket' expenses directly associated with it are assessed and the excess of the selling price over these expenses is the contribution to the total profits of the business.

There can be a real danger in introducing marginal profit products. This seemingly innocuous process often results in a business manufacturing the wrong product lines.

the marginal costing system

In the previous section reference was made to marginal costs operated in conjunction with a conventional costing system. This is quite different from the application of a marginal costing system which operates on a different principle from conventional costing in that it excludes fixed expenses in the calculation of product costs.

In the conventional costing system products are normally costed at full factory cost (including fixed expenses) and are included in stock at this amount until they are sold. As the goods are sold the corresponding factory costs are set against the sales value in the period profit statement. Administration and marketing expenses are usually charged as incurred in the profit statement for the period.

The marginal costing system charges only the variable factory costs to the product and this is the value taken into stock. The fixed factory expenses together with administration and marketing expenses are charged as incurred in the period profit statement.

Accountants are divided on the relative merits of the two systems and this can lead to management confusion. From the management viewpoint these are not alternative costing systems as each has a precise application and the system to be applied must be decided according to the particular conditions that apply in each business. A business cannot be forced into an accounting straightjacket.

Industrial progress has been marked by an increase in the investment in plant and machinery with the consequent increase in the fixed expenses proportion of total cost. In many industrial applications the control of volume is the vital factor in controlling the efficiency of the business. This factor can be appreciated by the very substantial loss of profit that a business can experience in a short period due to strike action. Maintaining the volume of output to protect the profits of the business and to give security of employment is the primary and one of the most important responsibilities of management and the accounting function must aid this task.

The marginal costing system can be effectively applied in those companies which manufacture hundreds, or even thousands, of different sizes of various products where the selling prices can be fixed without reference to product costs. Typical examples are pharmaceuticals, confectionery and cast iron pipe fittings where it would be usually impracticable to calculate product costs in the conventional manner.

The experience of one company, part of an international combine, with a large degree of autonomy, can illustrate the care that has to be exercised in applying the appropriate costing system. The company manufactured a fairly expensive product that was subject to seasonal demand. It was the leading product of its type and sales were steadily increasing. The product sold at a substantial profit. It was the practice of the company to operate at or near the maximum production capacity throughout the year and for a period of eight months on average there was heavy stockpiling of the finished product. During the four months of peak sales demand stocks were reduced to a nominal figure. The company was using conventional costs and the product was costed at full factory cost plus a proportion of administration and marketing expenses. This was the cost used for stock valuation.

The company became interested in the application of a marginal costing system and a thorough investigation was initiated with a view to applying it. Before reaching a final conclusion it was arranged that the monthly profit statements for the previous financial year should be re-drafted to show what the effect would be under a marginal costing system. The results were startling; for the first seven months of the financial year each monthly profit statement showed a loss, in the eighth month there was a small profit, in the remaining four months there were very substantial profits. The total profit for the financial year was substantial. The managing director refused to accept a system that was neither logical nor sensible and which if pursued would only provoke very serious repercussions from group headquarters.

A costing system must be judged in its application to each business and there can be no foregone conclusions; its practicability and accuracy in the particular conditions, its ability to present the facts in the right perspective, and last but not least—does it enable management to manage more effectively?

financial statements

The most important and influential statements in a business are the profit and loss account and the balance sheet: together these present a comprehensive view of the performance and the resources of the business. These statements are prepared monthly or four-weekly for management purposes, and annually to comply with statutory requirements.

The period profit and loss statement in outline usually takes the form shown in Figure 5. The budget figure shown on the statement may be based on the annual budget, or more probably on a short term budget. An alternative form of profit and loss statement which has proved to be helpful to some companies is shown in Figure 6. This statement is claimed to have two advantages:

1 It makes an important distinction between total sales and contributed sales.
2 It shows the relationship between production and sales as
   indicated by the increase or decrease in labour and overheads.
   The standard cost of production, less materials cost which is not
   a measure of productivity, is compared on the same basis with
   cost of sales to ascertain the increase or decrease to be shown.

PROFIT AND LOSS STATEMENT

Period _____

	This month		Period-to-date	
	Actual	Budget	Actual	Budget
	£	£	£	£
Sales				
Less cost of sales (factory)	___	___	___	___
Gross profit				
Variances: gain (or loss)	___	___	___	___
Factory operating profit				
Less technical expenses				
Less marketing expenses				
Less administration expenses	___	___	___	___
Operating profit				
Other income and expenditure	___	___	___	___
Profit before tax	___	___	___	___

Figure 5 Profit and loss statement

The balance sheet of a company is usually drawn up to show:

Liabilities	*Assets*
Share capital	Fixed assets including:
Reserves	Land and buildings
Bank overdraft	Plant and machinery
Long term loans	Current assets including:
Current liabilities including:	Stock
Trade creditors	Debtors
Other creditors	Cash

Certain important ratios can be established from these statements and the following are typical examples:

$$\frac{\text{Profit before tax}}{\text{Gross assets}} \qquad \frac{\text{Profit before tax}}{\text{Share capital}}$$

$$\frac{\text{Profit before tax}}{\text{Total sales}} \qquad \frac{\text{Profit before tax}}{\text{Contributed sales}}$$

$$\frac{\text{Total sales}}{\text{Inventory value}} \qquad \frac{\text{Total sales}}{\text{Working capital}}$$

Every company by design or circumstance uses fixed interest capital to supplement its resources. If the business is reasonably

PROFIT AND LOSS STATEMENT

Period _____

	This month		Period-to-date	
	Budget £	Actual £	Budget £	Actual £
1. Sales				
2. *Less* cost of materials	___	___	___	___
3. Contributed sales	___	___	___	___
4. Direct production costs				
5. Indirect production costs	___	___	___	___
6. Factory operating cost				
7. Adjust for labour and overheads in stock				
(*a*) Add decrease				
(*b*) Deduct increase	___	___	___	___
8. Net production cost	___	___	___	___
9. Factory contributed profit (3–9)				
10. *Less* technical expenses				
11. *Less* marketing expenses				
12. *Less* administration expenses	___	___	___	___
13. Net operating profit				
14. Other income and expenditure	___	___	___	___
15. Profit before tax	___	___	___	___

Figure 6 Profit and loss statement

successful this will have the effect of increasing the rate of return on equity capital. This balancing of finance is an important consideration.

summary

A business operates to plan and achieve certain basic and operational objectives which cannot be achieved without this planning and the influence and direction of management. Management planning will be concerned with long and short term objectives but each should be a link in a common chain, the only distinction being in the phasing of implementation. The annual budget is the general medium for translating long term plans and projects into sales and profit as they become due for implementation.

In the average business with the normal complexities, management can only plan effectively through management accounting: first, to project the results that can be expected from alternative courses of action, secondly to enable a decision to be made, and to provide the control information necessary for successful implementation.

Providing cost information as an aid to price-fixing or for interpreting selling prices, measuring the profitability of different products, providing a yardstick for measuring output, establishing profit/volume relationships; these are some of the more common applications of management accounting in addition to preparing profit statements and control information. Special investigations for particular purposes are also becoming a regular feature.

Management accounting operates through comparisons and to operate effectively two standards are generally required: performance standards, for example the method set for performing an operation and the time allowed for it, and operation standards related in the main to volume as determined by the operational budget. Management accounting can never be a standardised operation; it has its inherent problems, complexities, and controversies and these are enlarged by the complexity of business itself. Management has an important role in developing the management accounting function that will best suit the particular requirements of the business and it is no exaggeration to state that one will reflect the efficiency of the other.

Management must be better informed on its requirements for managing effectively. Efficiency-biased management will elevate the status and performance of the accounting function by providing the standards and information required for it to operate effectively. This will contribute immeasurably to the efficiency of management.

5 the sales budget

The planning of business objectives is still regarded more as a concept than a practice by many companies. In some companies it is looked upon as academic which indeed it will be if a company treats it academically. But given a realistic and factual approach a planning discipline will force a business to face up to the realities of its position —its strength and its weaknesses, its opportunities and its limitations— and will provide the guidelines to be followed in setting the right course to suit the business.

The object of planning objectives is to exert the maximum influence to optimize the performance of the business, and it constitutes the difference between managing and merely operating a business. Planning can be applied beneficially to any business regardless of size. The simple test is 'where management is necessary then planning is essential'. There should only be one comprehensive planning programme at any point of time but the phasing of the implementation of the different sections will, of course, vary. The planning programme can be broadly subdivided into two or three categories or segments:

THE LONG TERM PLAN This may cover a period of two to six years and will provide the basic or fundamental requirements of the business. Some of the considerations included in its survey are product policy and product design, markets and marketing policies, and production capacity. The entrepreneurial aspects of the business, product/market policies and strategy, will obviously be important factors in any long term plan. The long term plan is strategic in its implications and the success of the plan will largely condition the results attainable through operational planning.

OPERATIONAL PLANNING The operational plans translate the long term plans into sales and profit as they reach maturity and become due for implementation. The generally accepted period for operational planning is the financial year. Operational planning is concerned with the tactics and the methods to be adopted to exploit the capabilities of the business. The long term plan provides the products, the markets and the production facilities; the short term plan decides the actions to obtain the maximum volume of sales of the right product mix to satisfy the profit aim and to provide a balanced production programme. Operational planning is based initially on sales and ultimately on profit and it starts with a sales forecast which is translated into a sales plan and finally expressed as a sales budget.

THE PRODUCTION BUDGET OR SHORT TERM PLANNING In some companies the annual budget is an operating budget in that it determines not only the sales and profit budget but also the production budget. In many companies, however, it is not practicable to plan a production programme against an annual sales budget. In these cases the annual budget serves the essential purpose of assessing the sales and profit expectation; it projects the potential product sales in units and money, the cost of operating the business at this level of capacity, and the profit that should result. The production costs have to be taken into account to arrive at the total cost of operating the business but for this purpose only. The annual sales budget is not simply a statement of sales expectations but a sales programme for which the marketing division is fully responsible.

The production budget is normally based on the period adopted for the programming of production. Some companies do not operate through production programmes because the production planning function is not organised to this extent, and the company that makes a non-standard product will generally find it impracticable to programme production; in these cases the production budget is based on the period normally covered by the sales order book. The production budget projects the sales value of the production output, together with the production costs and these fix the responsibility of the production management and the standards against which its performance will be measured.

The annual budgeting procedure can be summed up as:

The annual budget places the responsibility on top management for achieving the profit objective and on the marketing division for meeting the sales programme. It can be the basis for product costing and inventory valuation.

The production budget sets the operating performance for the production division. It is not based on estimates but on a firm production programme or an established order book.

sales forecasting

A knowledge of the business and the industry in which it operates is a pre-requisite to any form of planning and a measure of the growth trend of the product and share of each market is likewise essential. The approach to sales forecasting is to decide what information is required and how it can be obtained; to analyse and evaluate the information and to group the facts emerging from this valuation into related patterns that can provide guidelines. In every stage judgement is necessary and it may be difficult if not impossible to obtain all the information or to establish all the facts. The number of variables and indeterminate factors add to the complexity of forecasting, but the company with three or more years experience can usually establish fairly reliable forecasts.

A sales forecast should provide the following information:

Sales by product lines, preferably in units and money.
Sales by territories.

Sales by customer classes where selling price varies by class.
Sales by month.

The sales forecaster uses data from several sources to project his sales forecast including:

Analysis of past sales.
Analysis of competitive and complementary industries.
Outside services.
Market analysis.
Field estimates.

ANALYSIS OF PAST SALES In analysing past sales it is usual to identify secular, cyclical, seasonal and random trends. Random trends being irregular and unpredictable have to be identified and eliminated to enable the other trends to be ascertained. The secular or long term trend shows the sales of the product line over an extended period and indicates its growth trend. The cyclical trend indicates the effect of general business conditions on sales. Monthly figures are more useful for this purpose and the influence of secular and seasonal trends must be eliminated to ascertain the cyclical trend. The forecaster will compare the cyclical trend of the product line with various published indices to find the index that gives the closest correlation. In some cases an index of business conditions in a particular field, for example, construction or agriculture or transport may provide the best guide. In establishing the index to be used 'lead' or 'lag' time has to be taken into account.

Probably the most difficult aspect of forecasting is to forecast business conditions. There is a risk in depending upon one set of figures or on the judgement of one individual and the forecaster may well obtain information from outside sources as a comparison and a guide.

ANALYSIS OF COMPETITIVE AND COMPLEMENTARY INDUS-TRIES A factor that cannot be overlooked by the forecaster is the competitive industries and their trend of growth and relative positions.

A forecast of sales of natural fibres must take into account the sales demand for the competing man-made fibres.

A study of the industries that are complementary to the product line can also provide essential information. The secular trend of the product line may be conditioned by the growth and development of closely related products. The third category of industries to be studied are the feeders or consumers of the product line whose secular trends can provide useful indicators; for example the motor car industry as a guide to steel, glass and instrument manufacturers, and the construction industry as a guide to steel, cement and building plant.

MARKET ANALYSIS The analysis of past sales provides essential information to the forecaster as trends are not likely to change frequently or rapidly, but nevertheless this does not constitute a dynamic approach to marketing. The progressive company will be out to increase its share of the markets and to decide upon the tactics to be adopted to best serve this purpose. Markets will be analysed to assess the sales potential, the type and impact of the competition, and the prevailing business conditions. Against this will be set the internal developments to strengthen the company competitively, the tactics to be adopted, and the share of the markets that should result. For most companies the analysis of markets will probably be best undertaken by the sales organisation.

FIELD ESTIMATES Estimates from the field sales force are an indispensable aid to sales forecasting. The trained sales representative being in direct contact with customers and potential customers should be favourably placed to assess the sales potential of his territory, the strength of the competition and the share of the market. The sales representative should be suitably trained to appreciate the information that is required, how it should be obtained and how it should be evaluated. This facet of sales representation has been neglected in the past and is only now receiving the attention it merits.

To ensure that field estimates are based on factual information some companies are now introducing standard procedures for sales estimating. The procedure is generally set in motion by the sales manager requesting field estimates from his area sales managers by a given date. This request may be accompanied by a statement setting out in general terms the expectations of the company; it may deal with trading conditions, growth trends of products, increasing share of markets and any particular sales aspects, and conclude by stating the percentage increase in sales expected in the budget year. Each area sales manager will request sales estimates from his sales representatives and will generally provide the guidelines to be followed in making the assessment. The sales representative will probably have a record of the sales to each customer in each of the previous three years. Every customer will be classified in any one of three or four grades according to the volume of sales. In one application customers were graded into three categories and the sales representative had to estimate the sales by products for each customer in grades A and B and the total sales for all customers collectively in grade C. The sales representative was expected to take particular measures to establish sales estimates for category A and reasonable measures for category B; the estimates for category C did not involve customer contacts. This approach is important as it is not unusual to find that in category A some 20 per cent of the total customers may account for 60 per cent or more of total sales; in category B, 50 per cent of the total customers may account for 30 per cent of total sales; and in category C the pattern may well be 30 per cent of customers for 10 per cent of sales.

The sales representative will submit his sales estimates to the area sales manager summarised in the categories mentioned above by product lines, together with the supporting detail. The area sales manager will examine the figures submitted by each representative and discuss, amend and finalize. He will then collate the sales estimates for all representatives and submit to the sales manager with any appropriate comments. The sales manager will receive the estimates from all the area sales managers and will examine, discuss, amend and finalize and then submit a summary of the estimates to the marketing director. Once the marketing director is satisfied with the sales estimates he will pass them to the forecaster for incorporation in the sales forecast.

SALES PLANNING It is sometimes difficult to make a clear distinction between sales planning and forecasting. Both are the function of the marketing director who will be responsible for submitting a sales plan for approval that commits the marketing division.

The sales plan will have to be examined from several viewpoints:

Does it utilise the production capacity?
Does it exceed the production capacity? If so is this because of total volume or is it that the sales mix imposes an unbalanced production mix?
Does the sales mix provide an acceptable profit target?

Once these conditions have been satisfied the sales plan is in effect a sales programme or sales budget imposing full responsibility on the marketing division for its achievement.

It is far from simple to provide a sales mix that will give the optimum profit and at the same time utilize the plant to the best advantage. A sales mix if not looked at from the factory point of view can impose an excess demand on certain units of the plant and an inadequate load on other units; in short an unbalanced production mix which results in low utilization of the production capacity. There is the other factor that the standard used for measuring the profitability of the different products may be unreliable, if not misleading. Profit related to total cost where a variety of products is involved may be quite misleading unless considered in conjunction with the proportion of the production capacity absorbed by each product. Planning the sales mix that will optimize profit is a logical and useful consideration but it has to be conditioned by the realities of the market situation, that is by total market demand and the marketability of the products.

As previously stated many companies are not in a position to implement an annual production programme based on an annual sales budget. These companies operate on a short term production budget based on a production programme or on the order book. Nevertheless if the sales order intake corresponds closely with the sales budget—which it is the responsibility of top management to ensure—then the same production output should be achieved through short term production budgets that would have been possible through an annual production budget. It is with this objective in view that the annual sales budget must be closely related to the production facilities to ensure that it provides the total volume and the right production mix to utilize the production capacity.

the sales budget

The sales budget should whenever practicable fix a sales quota for each sales representative against which his performance can be measured. The sales quotas for the representatives reporting to each area manager will in the aggregate show the performance required from the area manager and will be the measure of his achievement. The aggregate of the sales quotas for all areas will fix the responsibility of the sales manager. Figure 7 illustrates a typical form for comparing actual performance against budget. This same form can be used for the individual representative, or for the sales territories covered by each area manager, or for the business as a whole.

There are few things that are more important in a business than the sales plan as represented by the annual sales budget. The major weaknesses of a business should be exposed in formulating the sales plan and appropriate action should be taken to minimize their effect. But inefficiencies, basic or operating, that may have been overlooked in the sales planning are almost bound to be revealed in comparing the actual performance against the sales budget if this is factually pursued. Inefficiencies due to basic factors, for example a low market rating for a product, can only be corrected in the long term; operating inefficiencies, for example overdue deliveries to customers, can usually be corrected in the short term and within the budget period.

ORDERS RECEIVED

Area _____ Month_____ Representative·_____

Products	This month		Year-to-date		Last year
	Quota £	Actual £	Quota £	Actual £	Actual £
Total					

Figure 7 Budget and actual performance

It is fairly common for area sales managers to submit monthly sales reports to the sales manager commenting on the performance against budget and explaining the reasons for any failure. The sales manager submits a report to the marketing director who in turn presents his monthly report to the board of directors.

summary of business planning

Products and markets are the key entrepreneurial elements of a business and it is in connection with product-market policies and strategies that the most complex and fundamental issues have to be resolved. All forms of planning, long term, annual, or short term are dependent for their success on the sales outlet as provided by the annual sales budget. The long term objectives fulfil the purpose of the business and determine what it has to offer while the annual sales budget aims at customer acceptance. The annual sales budget ranks high in the planning of business objectives because it is centred on the customer and the contribution he makes to the continuance and growth of the business.

A business must see its sales income for the next three to five years and it must see this factually in terms of product lines, markets and volume of sales. It must know the growth trend of its product lines and when new models have to be introduced to maintain or enlarge its share of the market. If any product line is on the way out, or certain unprofitable lines have to be discontinued, it must see this in sufficient time to introduce a new product line, or to extend the markets for its existing lines, or to take whatever action is appropriate to maintain its volume of sales. Consideration must also be given to the production facilities to ensure that methods and equipment are kept up to date and in line with the prospective sales volume. These are some of the considerations that warrant long term planning.

For obvious reasons an annual sales budget can have little influence on long term considerations, for example it has to take the products as they are and make the most of them. The annual budget must recognise the competitive strengths and exploit them while minimizing the effect of weaknesses. The growth trend of the product, its market rating and its share of the market are essential information for sales planning. The market rating of the product and share of the market are not necessarily synonymous as a mediocre product may be bolstered up by efficient selling or vice versa. This is a factor that has to be closely examined.

In industrial selling it can be quite difficult to establish what the market is for a particular product. Some companies try to resolve this through advertising on a fairly wide scale and may supplement it by a close study of its existing customers A chemical company extended its sales at home and abroad through a close study of a selective range of customers; it ascertained the exact line of business of each customer and the product application. This study revealed certain applications for the product unknown to the company and a list of potential users was prepared for contact by the technical sales representatives. This can be a constructive approach; who are our leading customers and what is their exact line of business?; what companies are engaged in these lines of business that are not customers? Sometimes it is left to the sales representatives to make new contacts but this can be more effectively planned and organised through the head office.

Tactics are important in the implementation of the sales budget. The marketing function has fewer principles and guidelines than most other functions and for this reason probably offers wider scope for ingenuity.

As previously mentioned some of the major decisions of a business are concerned with products and markets. There must be a factual approach to decision-making. Alfred P. Sloan Junior, who had to make many major decisions during his long term as chief executive of General Motors advocated the need to establish the facts and circumstances in the knowledge that the final act in making a decision is intuitive. In every major consideration management never has all the facts and information to make an automatic decision; judgement and the uncertainty of the future cannot be wholly eliminated from the decision-making process. It is in this setting that business objectives have to be planned.

It has frequently been stated that a business should be marketing oriented. It might be nearer the mark to say a business should be product/market oriented. Nevertheless, every function, department and section of a business should be assigned a specific objective in harmony with the total objective of the business. The period or time span of the objective cannot be fixed for the business as a whole but has to be related to the function and the circumstances. The long term objectives decide what the business is, or will be, and what it has to offer, while the annual budget translates this into sales income, expenditure and profit. In the event that an annual budget is impracticable for the production division, a logical and rational period for the programming of production to satisfy customer requirements has to be decided and this sets the basis for the production budget. Long term, annual and short term planning have to be geared to the particular conditions and requirements of each business.

Planning through budgets has a built-in feed-back system giving a constant comparison between actual and budgeted performance and as differences are highlighted management has the option of applying pressure or revising the plan at its discretion. Companies that rely upon *ad hoc* planning for managing the business do not as a rule have the advantages of a feed-back system and consequently serious delays can occur before corrective action is taken.

Who makes the planning decisions and how are these decisions made? In the large company there will probably be a planning committee which submits its recommendations to the chief executive. In the smaller company the committee will probably comprise certain executives who will meet as required under the chairmanship of the chief executive. What every business needs is a system of management which will determine, amongst other things, the planning procedure and the planning periods.

The fundamental requirement of every business is to survive and this means maintaining its profit earnings. The gateway to profit is sales and the business must, therefore, maintain its sales volume. The foundation of sales volume is products and markets which should be expressed as a product/market policy. The question therefore arises— if any change is required in product or market policy to generate the required volume of sales how long will it take to implement the change? For many companies this period will be fixed by the time required by the product design department to design a new model or a new product. According to the type of product the minimum period may be three years and in some cases very much longer and this sets the time span of long term planning.

In general, long term planning starts with the marketing division which has to project sales performance for the planning period. Market intelligence should provide a continuous check on the projected performance as a number of factors can upset the calculations. The growth trend of each major product line in each market, the impact of competition both direct and indirect, the market rating of the product and share of the market, and technological developments, are some of the factors that should be constantly reviewed.

Other factors apart the long term plan should be systematically studied every year.

The character of the business, what it is and what it should be, is determined by long term planning. How to make the most of what the business is becomes the province of annual and short term budgeting.

6   the production budget

A distinction has to be recognised in the purposes that a production budget can serve. In general terms a production budget fulfils two major purposes:

1 As a means of assessing cost of production. In the over-all assessment of the prospects of the business for the following financial year—an essential operation where the object is to manage the business rather than to be content with simply operating it—the projected sales have to be translated into production costs as a means of calculating the potential profit. Dependent upon the product line and the market standing and resources of the business the annual sales budget may be the basis for planning and programming production, that is for preparing an annual operating budget. But it will probably be impracticable for the majority of companies to plan so far in advance in view of the uncertainties and risks involved, and a short term operational production budget is the logical procedure.

2 To plan production through a short term operational budget. The short term operational budget may cover a period of anything from one month up to six months. It should be based on the programming period where production is programmed, or failing this, on the normal period covered by the order book.

The company manufacturing non-standard products has to base its production plan on the average period of the order book.

stability of production

Stability of production is an important factor in the profitable operation of a business as fixed expenses now constitute such a large proportion of total production costs that a reduction in output can only be offset by a comparatively small reduction in expenditure. The aim must be to stabilize production at, or above, an economic level that will both guarantee the profitable operation of the business and provide security of employment. Anything less than this, whatever the reason, will be a reflection on the efficiency of the management.

Stability of production stems in the first place from the marketing division in providing the volume of orders necessary to make this possible. The marketing division may provide the necessary volume of orders over a period but can never guarantee an order intake at a regular and consistent level and management has to establish the means of counteracting this ebb and flow. The procedure to be adopted depends upon the type of product: standard or non-standard.

STANDARD PRODUCTS The company manufacturing standard products has the advantage that it can maintain production at a steady level through producing for stock as a means of equalising a fluctuating order intake. It is not always appreciated, however, that stability of production and minimum inventories are not compatible. The resources of the business will be a factor in deciding how far inventories can be increased to maintain the production level.

NON-STANDARD PRODUCTS The manufacturers of non-standard products do not have the advantage of a finished goods inventory to equalize the order intake; their safeguard is to operate through reliable indicators that will give adequate warning of a probable reduction in the order intake to enable the appropriate action to be taken.

Statistics can be an important guide to indicate probable trends in the order book. One highly successful company maintained monthly records showing the value of quotations sent out, the value of orders obtained against quotations and the value of repeat orders. Over a period of years the company had developed a sound basis for evaluating the orders that would result from the quotations sent out, and the probable time lag. As a guide for this evaluation customers were classified according to the prospects of obtaining their orders and this classification was updated periodically in line with current experience. The evaluation of orders from quotations could vary from 100 down to 20 per cent for customers, with an average of 10 per cent for non-customers. The analyst was fairly accurate in forecasting the trend of orders.

The action taken to offset a probable decline in orders was two-fold; a reduction in the prices quoted for an appropriate period with an intensive follow-up where there were reasonable prospects of an order and concentration on selected customer contacts using the classification previously mentioned. The experience of the company was that timely reductions in quoted prices need only be small but that delayed reductions had to be substantial as it was then common knowledge in the trade that less work was available.

production systems

The function of the production division is to provide the products in the required quantity at the required time by the best and most economical production methods. The first stage of this process is to define the product in a manner that can be understood and acted upon by the production division. The design and product development sections have to define the product and this may vary from a simple specification to a mass of drawings, each drawing detailing a single part and specifying the materials to make it, and the whole being summarised in a general arrangement drawing. Given the product specification the technical section, production methods or production engineering, has to decide the methods of production and provide the necessary production facilities of the right type and in the right quantity to meet the anticipated volume of output. In process or flow production the type and size of plant incorporates these factors; here the method of production is built into the plant. In continuous or mass production the conditions are somewhat similar with the methods of production being largely incorporated in special purpose machines.

The important feature of these two systems of production is that the methods have been geared to the particular requirements of the product and the volume of output. In batch production where it is fairly common for several sizes of the same product, or several different products, to be produced using common production facilities there is much less scope for specialization and the consquence is that the production requirements are not as a rule closely studied. In batch production the methods are not built into the machine since general-purpose machines are largely used and the methods have therefore to be recorded on operations layout sheets. It is necessary also to know the operating times in batch production and these are shown on the operations layout sheets.

Producing the required quantity of the product at the required time is a function of production planning and control. In process and particularly continuous production there may be difficulties in obtaining materials and parts from the suppliers by the due dates but once these are available the production control function is relatively straightforward. In batch production of all but the simplest products production planning and control is in every aspect a complex function.

Every production unit is unique in some respect; it may be in its product range, in its plant, in its methods, or in its organization, but the fact remains that no two are identical, not even factories controlled by the one company and making identical products. It follows that the production system should be geared to the particular conditions and requirements. Process and continuous production systems achieve this objective but in batch production the systems are not generally particularized. For example in batch manufacture of the assembly type of product the system generally applied is to purchase and produce parts on a maximum-minimum stock replacement basis. All parts large or small, expensive or inexpensive, are dealt with in a similar manner. Work load records invariably show the work load against each machine or group in respect of all parts without making any distinction between the important and the relatively unimportant parts.

The efficiency of batch production systems can be judged by the extent that the principles of continuous or line production are applied insofar as the product and the conditions permit. Every system starts with an appreciation of the characteristics of the product. In most products it generally follows that a few principal parts account for a large proportion of the total cost of the product and these should be singled out for special consideration. Some of these considerations are:

Can any of the principal parts be line produced economically? The question here is whether the reduction in inventory and the saving in cost will justify the additional investment in plant.

Can the purchase of principal parts be arranged against a delivery schedule? This can reduce inventories.

Can principal parts which cannot be line produced be given priority in the work load? This can improve production planning and promote dependable deliveries. The principal parts are scheduled against a strict time schedule and the assembly programme is planned accordingly. The minor parts are controlled on a maximum-minimum basis to be available to meet the assembly programme.

production planning

An important factor to be recognised is that production planning in all but the simplest applications is a skilled operation that requires a systematic and organised approach. Its importance to the efficiency of a business should not be underestimated and the would-be successful company has to ensure that it has not only the right system for its operations but that the organisation has the skills that the system imposes.

The short term production budget, which is the planning basis applicable to most companies, aims at producing the products in the required quantity at the required time and at the minimum cost. The period of the short term production budget should be based on the production programme which in turn reflects the throughput time, or production cycle time, of the products. This may vary with each product and the objective should be to find the least common denominator. In process and continuous production programming is relatively simple since the production cycle time is established in installing the plant. In batch production the conditions and operating times are not so determinate but nevertheless programming can be effectively established if it is centred on the principal parts.

The short term budget is the basis for determining the labour requirements and procurement and for measuring actual performance against planned performance.

LABOUR REQUIREMENTS The annual production budget will indicate the size of the labour force required but the actual number to be employed, that is the head-count, will be determined by the short term budget. If the budget indicates that more labour is required then the prospect of recruiting it has to be taken into account. If the budget shows that less labour is required the question of increasing stock to avoid redundancy has to be considered.

PROCUREMENT Materials and purchased parts required to meet the budget have to be scheduled. Some companies advise suppliers of their probable requirements on an annual basis or may place actual orders for a year's supply. In these cases the short term budget is used as a delivery schedule. Where actual purchase orders have to be placed against the budget then the lead time has to be established to ensure that the production programme is planned far enough in advance to permit the supplies to be available in time to meet production requirements.

MEASURING PERFORMANCE For many companies the calendar month, or a four-weekly period, is appropriate for comparing the results achieved with the budget. In the assembly type of product where batch production is extensively applied the assembly programme is the basis for comparison, and this can apply even where the product takes longer than one month to assemble and whether it is standard or non-standard.

It is important to appreciate the real function of a short term budget. In cases where a monthly budget applies the purpose that it serves is generally nothing more than a measure of planned output; it is often based on an assembly programme and shows what has been assembled as compared with the plan. It is a useful control to ensure that the planned output is achieved and translated into sales but it does not fulfil the purpose of a short term budget. A short term budget is a complete production plan in miniature. It is the basis for planning and controlling production expenses, for determining the number of production personnel to be employed, and obtaining the purchased materials and parts required: all in relation to the planned output. It has its limitations in that a short term budget would not normally influence the production organization or the number of salaried employees which are usually longer term considerations, but it would determine the number of direct and indirect workers. The production budget should, of course, provide for a continuous check on output. Every company has to consider the policy of planning production through a short term budget; unless, of course, it has the conditions and the resources to plan through an annual operating budget.

production costs

A budget must project a reasonable level of efficiency and this will be reflected in the production costs. The considerations previously mentioned—production stability, finding the right production system in line with the characteristics of the products and the volume of output, a production planning organization that has the skills appropriate to the demands of the product and planning through an operating budget—are some of the more important aids to improving efficiency and reducing costs. Other important considerations are the methods of production and the establishment of performance standards, and the class and condition of the production plant.

The procedure for calculating production costs is much the same for an annual and a short term budget; in the former it is based on an approved annual sales budget and in the latter on a production programme or on the order book. The important factor necessary for projecting production costs is the quantity to be produced of each product.

It is important to identify the structure or anatomy of production costs. Process production provides a good example. Here the plant is specially designed to produce a single product and the costs are easily identified. First there are the costs directly related to the plant itself which comprise depreciation, maintenance, the cost of floor space and power. There is no particular difficulty in estimating these costs. Depreciation is written off in equal annual instalments spread over the estimated life of the plant. Maintenance costs can be closely estimated where a preventive maintenance procedure is in operation; the materials cost, particularly the cost of critical expensive parts, is generally known, and the labour force is closely geared to the planned requirement. The cost of floor space comprises repairs to buildings, heating, lighting, rent, rates and insurance, and these expenses are usually combined under the caption of establishment charges and generally expressed as a cost per square foot. The cost chargeable to the plant will be based on the area occupied. Power cost can be easily calculated.

Secondly there is the labour cost directly associated with production which will include the feeding of the raw materials into the plant and the packing of the finished product. Thirdly there is the cost of the raw material entering into the product. In process production this is usually expressed as the yield of finished product that can be obtained from a given quantity of raw material.

Those three costs are the direct costs of production. Any incidental labour controlled by the plant supervisor and any general expenses incurred by the department are classed as the indirect production costs. Costs incurred outside the production department but within the production division are generally classed as service costs.

In engineering products the classification is more complex but the same principles apply:

1 DIRECT PRODUCTION COSTS
  a Plant operating costs. These will include depreciation, maintenance, floor space, power and the cost of tools and other supplies.
  b Direct labour costs. These will include the machine operators and setters.
  c Direct materials cost. These will comprise the cost of all materials and purchased parts entering into the product.

2 INDIRECT PRODUCTION COSTS These will include the general labour and expenses of the production departments.

3 PRODUCTION SERVICES COSTS These will comprise the costs of providing the essential services to production and will include stores, inspection, methods engineering, planning and production control and personnel and purchasing if these are contained in the production function. In some companies the production service costs are sub-divided as between services and administration.

It is customary in the manufacture of standard engineering products to operate two documents for instruction and guidance: an assembly parts list showing the parts necessary to assemble the finished product, and an operations layout for each part to be manufactured and for assembly. The operations layout lists every operation on the part and shows against it the machine group or production centre performing it and the allowed time. It also shows the materials required to produce it. From this basic data the materials cost of the product and the operating hours for each production centre to produce it can be established. These unit figures are multiplied by the quantity to be produced of the product and the aggregate of all products gives the total materials cost and the total operating hours by production centres. The operating hours of each production centre are translated into man hours by applying an established performance factor; the man hours are increased to allow for normal idle time and other considerations and then converted into the number of operators and setters required by each production centre and in total; the direct labour cost is computed by applying the appropriate wage rates. This procedure provides a basis for establishing standard costs as well as budgeted costs.

Figure 8 illustrates a short term budget. Following the normal

SALES AND PRODUCTION PROFIT BUDGET
Period 16 weeks: periods _____   This period _____

Budget total 16 weeks £	Particulars	This period		Cumulative	
		Budget £	Actual £	Budget £	Actual £
	Sales *Less* materials cost				
	Contributed sales				
	Direct production costs Indirect production costs Service departments cost Production administration costs				
	Total operating costs				

	Adjustment for labour and
	    overheads in stock
	        Add decrease
	        Deduct increase				

	Production cost of sales				
	Production profit				

Figure 8 Sales and production profit budget

procedure the budget figures would be sub-divided into four-weekly or monthly figures according to the frequency required for comparing actual and budgeted results.

The short term budget although it may be loosely described as a production budget is in fact a sales and profit budget. The emphasis is on production because it is not generally based on a sales forecast but on the known facts established by a production programme or an order book. The form of presentation of a short term budget can vary considerably. Figure 8 is not a common form of presentation; it was designed to meet the requirements of a group of engineering companies which attached particular importance to certain factors:

1 CONTRIBUTED SALES The materials content in each product varied considerably and it was considered that profit should be measured against the contribution of the business rather than against total sales.

2 TOTAL PRODUCTION COSTS It was considered that the total costs of the production division, suitably classified under the functional sub-divisions should be shown, notwithstanding that a standard costing system was in operation. This distinction will be apparent when considering the standard form of short term budget shown in Figure 9.

SALES AND PRODUCTION PROFIT BUDGET

Period 16 weeks: periods _____   This period _____

Budget total 16 weeks £	Particulars	This period		Cumulative	
		Budget £	Actual £	Budget £	Actual £

	Sales
	Less cost of sales
	
	Gross profit
	
	Variances:
	  Materials cost: add (or deduct)
	  Direct labour costs: add (or deduct)
	  Factory overheads: add (or deduct)				

	Net production profit				

Figure 9 Sales and production profit budget

3 STOCK ADJUSTMENT FOR LABOUR AND OVERHEADS IN STOCK The difference in the labour and overheads in work-in-progress, finished parts and finished products stock, at the beginning and end of the period shows whether the total production costs were sufficient to produce the sales or whether value was withdrawn or added to the stock. This is an important factor as it shows whether the contributed sales are at the right level to absorb the production costs.

4 DIRECT PRODUCTION COSTS Particular importance was attached to the segregation of the direct costs as these in total were regarded as the measure of production capacity in the absence of a natural unit of output. These were also regarded as a suitable yardstick for keeping the other production expenditure in the right perspective.

Figure 9 illustrates a form of budget presentation that is fairly commonly adopted, particularly where a standard costing system applies. The products budgeted and sold during the period are costed at standard material costs and standard production costs and the gross profit established accordingly. The gross profit is then adjusted for variances from the standard costs to show the net production profit.

The procedure so far has been centred on the manufacture of standard products. Manufacturers of non-standard or jobbing products with a varying materials content are not generally in a position to forecast total sales. Here the proper approach is to focus the budget on the production organisation and the production costs; an assessment is then made of the costs of operating the other divisions and of the profit that should be earned, and the aggregate of these figures gives the contributed sales. An estimate may be made of the probable materials cost and added to the contributed sales to arrive at total sales, but this figure is not significant since it does not decide the profit. In submitting price quotations profit will be calculated on the contributed sales figure and the materials cost added to give the selling price.

standard costs and their implication

It goes without saying that standard costs should reflect a reasonable degree of efficiency both in performance and in the level of activity. It is not unusual to find that the process of preparing and introducing a standard costing system does in fact add to the efficiency of a business. Standard costs, however, even though they may be closely worked to in practice, are not the final testament to the efficiency of a business as they do not generally provide any criteria for measuring the basic efficiencies. Is the design of the product too costly? Is the sales demand for the product and, therefore, the volume of production, too low in relation to competitors to justify the production methods and plant that are available to them? These are some of the basic considerations that lie deeper than standard costing and this limitation has to be recognised.

the monthly production budget

One of the problems that can face many companies is not so much a question of gearing the production costs to the output but of ensuring that the output is forthcoming for the expenditure that is being incurred. Given a satisfactory order book with an adequate production labour force, management has to obtain the output warranted by the expenditure to ensure the profits and to give reliable deliveries to customers. It has to ensure efficient planning and proper implementation. It is with this object in view that many companies operate a monthly or four-weekly budget.

Figure 10 shows a simple form of four-weekly production budget. In one engineering company operating a four-weekly budget the procedure was to issue the budget by the third working day showing the sales budgeted for the current period with a comparison of the results achieved in the previous period. Assembly work was planned against an assembly programme and it usually required two weeks after completion of assembly for despatch. This was the basis of the

P.P.C.—8

SALES AND PRODUCTION BUDGET

Four weekly period _____

Products	Previous period				Budget this period	
	Budget		Actual			
	Quantity	Sales value	Quantity	Sales value	Quantity	Sales value
Total						

Figure 10 Four-weekly sales and production budget

budget. Management knew the output that was required each period in accordance with the order book and anything less shown in the budget raised an immediate enquiry. Likewise any failure to implement the budget was investigated. It was an essential exercise for management and men.

summary

No two manufacturing concerns are alike and the production system must be geared to the special circumstances of the business. The limitations imposed by the products and the volume of production have to be recognised but within these limits the opportunity should be taken of exploiting any possibilities. The most fruitful field for the application of this principle is probably in the batch manufacture of engineering products. Obviously the product is made in batches because the volume of production does not warrant a continuous production system. But while this may be true for the product as a whole it may not be true for all its parts. In most products a few parts will probably account for the bulk of the cost and these parts should be singled out for special study and treatment. It is action of this kind that can improve production, simplify production planning and reduce costs.

The aim of every business should be to stabilize production through consolidated growth. Failure to stabilize production can be a very expensive operation which management has to make every effort to avoid.

Performance and operating standards should be set as a basis for deciding the expenditure that should be incurred and as a means of controlling excesses. Standard costs should be fixed wherever practicable. The production costs should be arranged by functions: the costs of the production departments sub-divided between the direct and indirect costs, the cost of the services departments and the administration costs.

The problem that is most common in business is not, as so often quoted, that of gearing costs to production but of obtaining the output warranted by the costs. Failure to obtain the required output can be influenced, if not entirely eliminated, by competent planning and effective supervision.

7 profit and capital budgets

The purpose of a business is to earn profit but it is doubtful if any highly successful business has been created solely through the profit motive. In his book 'The Will to Manage', Marvin Bower quotes a statement by President Calvin Coolidge which aptly sums up the situation: 'No enterprise can exist for itself alone. It ministers to some great need, it performs some great service, not for itself, but for others; or failing therein it ceases to be profitable and ceases to exist.'

Profit cannot be ignored since it is both a measure of the success of the business and the means of its survival and growth. Corporate planning—long term, medium, and short term—and its accomplishments are reflected sooner or later in the annual profit and loss statement and balance sheet. Effective management ensures that the long term plans are adequate for the needs of the business, that there is proper operational direction and control for their implementation as this falls due, and that the results shown in the annual profit and loss statement reflect the planned level of efficiency. The efficiency of a business is determined by its market rating, that is by its share of the markets that provide the sales outlets for its products. The first task of a business is to protect its sales income through its product/market policies and strategy, reinforced by a research and product design division with the appropriate technological skills and a competent marketing organisation. For most industrial concerns these require long term planning.

Management must have a clear understanding of the profit factors. It must recognise the basic factors that are long term considerations that have to be thought out two to five years in advance and the operational factors that fall within the compass of the financial year and can have an immediate impact on the annual trading results, for example, the income and how it will be obtained and the major cost areas.

the system of management

A system of management imposes disciplinary action on all members of an organization from the chief executive downwards. Obviously top management must determine and accept the disciplines that are essential for efficient operation of the business and translate these into procedures and practices for the guidance of the members of the organization. General Motors operates through a policy of decentralized operations and responsibilities with centralized policies and co-ordinated control thus providing scope for individual initiative and freedom of action within a broad framework of guidance and restraint. Although essential in the large company a system of management is, nevertheless, important for the smaller company in forcing it to recognise and apply the principles of management appropriate to its operations.

A system of management embraces principles, policies, objectives, strategy, operational programmes, procedures and standards of performance. The principles of efficient operation are well known and are not the prerogative of any one company; what management has to do is to adapt these principles to the particular needs of the business and to incorporate them in a system of management.

Policies are a set of rules for the operation of the business and perhaps the most important is that which defines the nature of the business. Henry Ford decided upon a policy of making a cheap car for the masses and this inevitably decided the nature of the business. In most companies it is not the nature of the business that decides the products but the other way round. In many cases it is rational to start with the product/market policy. It was the product/market policy first considered by General Motors in 1921 that contributed significantly to the success of the company and defined the nature of the business. The policy reduced the number of lines and provided a car in each price area from the lowest to the highest quality that could be quantity produced.

Having through the product/market policy decided the nature of the business, the next stage is to plan the objectives and the strategy for making the policy work and this may embrace a number of factors, for example, research and development, sales and distribution, general selling price structure and discount terms, and production policy. At any point of time these may be long term plans or they may be emerging from the process of long term planning and ready for operating. At the operational stage they should be incorporated in the annual budget plan.

Many companies accept the need to introduce procedures and practices and to set standards of performance but few by comparison acknowledge the necessity of a planning discipline. It is a commonly expressed view that a company should consider periodically what its business is and what it should be. In fact this would be regularly reviewed in the most practical manner by the business that operates a planned programme. Once a year at least a business should assess what its sales income will be in the next three to five years in terms of major product lines and major markets or market segments. The futurity will be dependent upon such factors as the time required to modify the design of an existing product or to introduce a new product, or to improve or enlarge its production facilities, or extend or change its marketing policies and methods, all of which can be long term. Unless a business can be reasonably sure of at least maintaining its sales income in the foreseeable future then action is necessary.

Each major product line must be studied in relation to each major market. If the product line has a growth potential the rate of growth should be established. The impact of direct and indirect competition and other outside forces should be assessed in conjunction with any plans the business may have for strengthening its competitive position and an opinion be formed of share of the market. If there is a diminishing demand for a major product line—perhaps through the introduction of an alternative product which is capturing the market —then the business must decide if this can be compensated by stepping up the sales of its other product lines or by introducing another product. Manufacturers of iron pipe fittings and iron pipes are now faced by competition from plastics which will increase as the technology develops. Plastics require a different manufacturing technique and if the manufacturers of pipe fittings elected to go into plastics their production plant, represented in the main by iron foundries, would be useless for this purpose. Obviously their aim will be to introduce products that can utilize the existing production capacity; they will probably change their product lines but not necessarily their business which is ironfounding.

A business has to be satisfied that its long term planning encompasses the needs of the business and that its operational activities are efficiently organized as these will directly influence the profits earned in the financial year. The purpose of the annual budget is to weigh up the strong and the weak points of the business in relation to its opportunities and to decide the tactics to exploit its strength and minimize its weakness. The annual plan or budget is being adopted by an increasing number of companies but the general state of the art has not attained a high level of proficiency because often it lacks the authority and the responsibility of a planning discipline. It is generally accepted that the success of an operation is a measure of the thought and care given to it before its commencement; this is the object of a planning discipline—to ensure that plans are formulated in a systematic, factual and rational manner and are as sound as human ingenuity can make them. Many a company has established a successful business by nothing more complicated than putting widely known principles to work consistently and well.

The system of management and its processes extend the participation in the running of the business. It enables responsibility to be delegated to a lower level in the management structure and nearer to the action and the facts. In this environment a foreman can virtually act as a manager in his department thus beneficially improving his status and his contribution. It is a basis that can enable common people to do uncommon things.

In an organized business everyone in the organization from the foreman upwards knows his position and his duties and responsibilities. This is all part of the management system. Proper planning implemented by a budgetary procedure adds another element and that is accountability. In conformity with the total aims of the business, individual tasks are set which show what is required and how performance will be measured. The annual budget imposes a definite responsibility on the marketing director for which he is accountable, but accountability also extends down to the sales representative through his sales quota. In a similar manner the production director is accountable for the production budget, annual or short term, and this accountability extends to the foreman of each department through his sectional budget. This procedure extends to every facet of the business. Profit planning can be more effective when it is supported by a management system and a management programme that sets individual tasks with accountability for performance. It is an essential aid in building a successful business and in developing personalities.

the profit budget and its aims

The annual profit budget may be an assessment of what the business can be expected to do operating at a reasonable level of efficiency and fully exploiting its opportunities, or it may be an operational budget that sets specific tasks with accountability for performance.

In some companies a year is a relatively short period for profit planning and the annual budget is, therefore, an operational budget; the annual sales budget is translated into a production budget which then becomes the basis for programming purchases and manufacture;

the cost of materials and the cost of operating the production division and the other divisions of the business are summarized and set against the sales income to establish the profit aim. This defines the contribution to be made by each division and department and fixes the accountability for performance.

The majority of companies will not find it practicable to programme production against an annual sales budget. In these cases the annual budget provides an assessment only of the prospects facing the business. But as an assessment it generally imposes standards of performance with accountability on all divisions other than the production division; top management is accountable for the profit target; the marketing division is accountable for the annual sales budget and its costs of operation; the administrative or financial division is accountable for its budgeted costs; the technical division is accountable for implementing the programme laid down within the limits of its cost budget. The production division is accountable through its short term budget for performance and operating costs. In short the annual contribution of the production division may be represented by two, three, or possibly four, short term budgets as against one budget for the other divisions.

the profit factors

The factors that influence the profits of a business can be generally classed as basic or operational.

BASIC FACTORS The basic factors are the marketability of the products and the markets established as sales outlets and the sales potential. These will be generally reflected in the volume of sales and are an indication of the efficiency of product design and marketing competence. Product design has a major influence in two ways: it influences the sales through the quality and suitability of the product and it basically fixes the cost of production. A design that minimizes materials cost and simplifies the methods of production is a key profit factor. Marketing is important in providing a profile of the product for the guidance of the design and in establishing markets and promoting sales.

Volume of sales is extremely important in its effect on costs and profit. Volume can have a basic influence on production costs in promoting or restricting the application of the best manufacturing methods with the best plant and equipment. A manufacturer limited by volume to batch production on general-purpose machines cannot hope to compete successfully with a competitor whose sales volume justifies continuous production on specialized machinery.

OPERATIONAL FACTORS The operational factors relate to current operations and the costs incurred in the general running of the business. One way to control these costs is to identify and segregate the significant and the relatively insignificant items. The former will be individually controlled to ensure that the cost is maintained at a minimum level whereas the less significant items with similar characteristics will be grouped and controlled as a group. If at any time the group cost appears to be excessive then it is analysed in detail. Another common method is to group the related costs and if any appears to be excessive then reference can be made to the group summary statement showing the individual items. As previously mentioned the cost of operating the production division may be subdivided into the following groups:

1 Cost of operating the production departments:
a Direct.
b Indirect.

2 Cost of services departments.

3 Cost of production administration.

This may be extended to include:

4 Cost of operating the marketing division:
a Selling.
b Distribution.

5 Cost of operating the financial division:
a Finance and control.
b General offices.
c General administration.

The groups and the sub-division of each group will depend on the size and the requirements of the business. If details of any group cost are required they can be obtained from the group statement listing the itemized costs. It has to be appreciated that a cost may be significant but largely fixed and, therefore, not responsive to control. Conversely a relatively insignificant but variable cost may be highly significant in its implications. A company operating at full plant capacity with no available space for additional machines decided that the one way to increase profit was to concentrate on reducing costs. A 10 per cent reduction was the aim where the cost was large enough to justify a worthwhile saving. The smaller costs, which included direct labour, were excluded from the investigation in the belief that the possible savings did not warrant the work involved. At a later date, and for a different reason, the direct labour costs had to be investigated in relation to the allowed times for production operations, which formed the basis for payment by results. The investigation showed that the allowed times were not a true reflection of the work and effort involved, some being too high and others too low. The times were amended and resulted in a 10 per cent increase in productivity from the same labour force with only a comparatively small increase in the labour costs.

product mix

A variety of products can add to the complexity of operating the business unless there are separate production facilities for each product which is the exception rather than the rule. The marketing division may be able to project a fairly reliable sales forecast for each product that averages out in the course of the year. But from the viewpoint of production programming which generally operates on a short term cycle, annual averages are seldom an aid to planning. In one company which programmed production six times a year it was found that the plan of the product mix varied each time although at the end of the year it all averaged out. It is for this reason that companies cannot generally base their production programme on an annual sales budget; first because there is no guarantee that it will average out, and secondly, as shown above, a plan based on an average is never in line with customer demands at any point of time. It could be argued that inventories should be able to compensate for these variations but this is usually impracticable with a variety of product. The complexity of production planning can, however, be greatly simplified in these circumstances as mentioned earlier by concentrated planning on the major parts with *ad hoc* planning through minimum-maximum stocks of the minor parts.

Changes in the product mix can often have a marked effect on sales and profit and it is, therefore, important to establish the most profitable mix and to plan the sales effort accordingly. Needless to add, however, selling the ideal product mix is the most difficult operation in almost every business.

In estimating the effect of a varying product mix a factor of primary importance is the profitability of each product, which is usually measured by relating the total cost of the product to the selling price. It is not unusual to find in comparing the costs of the products that the largest difference between them is the materials cost. This is an important factor for the business which believes that profit should be related only to the contribution made by the business. In this connection contributed sales, which is total sales less materials cost, is regarded as the measure and the reward of the business contribution. The costs to be set against the contributed sales are those incurred in operating the business, sometimes termed added costs, as the materials cost has already been excluded. This can be carried a stage further by stating that the contribution made by a business is to convert purchased materials into saleable products and that profit should, therefore, be related to the conversion cost which may be interpreted as the direct production costs, excluding materials and all the other costs of operating the business. All these methods will present a different slant on the profitability of each product as was shown in the section on management accounting.

Obviously a business must be fairly certain of the profitability of each product or it may push the wrong product mix. Providing a business is aware of the different methods of determining the profitability of a product it can make the decision that suits its conditions and opinion. It will not be in the position of a little knowledge being dangerous.

the profit statement

A common form of presenting a profit budget is shown in Figure 11. As previously stated this will be prepared annually and also for interim periods where short term production budgets are in operation. An alternative form of profit budget is shown in Figure 12. The advantage, if any, of the alternative procedure is to measure the extent that the sales for the period have been matched by the production for the period.

Budgets can vary considerably in their presentation and contents. Probably the most common form is that shown in Figure 11 but there are variations in this presentation as illustrated, for example, in Figure 13. This presentation is more limited in its application since it requires standard products and a standard costing system, but where

ANNUAL SALES AND PROFIT BUDGET
for the financial year ending _____   Period _____

Annual budget £	Particulars	This period		Year-to-date	
		Actual £	Budget £	Actual £	Budget £
	Sales				
	Cost of sales				
	Gross profit				
—	Variances: gain (or loss)				
—	Materials				
—	Direct labour				
—	Production overheads				
	Production operating profit				
	Technical expenses				
	Selling and distribution expenses				
	General administration expenses				
	Net operating profit				

Figure 11 Annual sales and profit budget

SALES AND PROFIT BUDGET
period _____

Annual budget		Particulars	This period		Year-to-date	
Annual total £	Year-to-date £		Budget £	Actual £	Budget £	Actual £
1	2	3	4	5	6	7
		Sales				
		Less materials cost				
		Contributed sales				
		Direct production costs				
		Indirect production costs				
		Services costs				
		Production administration costs				
		Total operating costs				
		Adjust for labour and overheads in stock: decrease or (increase)				
		Cost of sales				
		Production profit contribution				
		Costs: technical division				
		Costs: selling and distribution				
		Costs: general administration				
		Net trading profit				

Figure 12 Sales and profit budget

these conditions apply, Figure 13 has advantages in that it shows the analysis of sales by products and the profit on each product.

The presentation shown in Figure 12 can be usefully applied where short term budgets are operated in conjunction with the annual budget. One business using this form had a forward order book averaging five months and in operating its half-yearly budget it had only to forecast its order intake for the sixth month. It operated on the basis of two four-weekly periods and a five-weekly period to make up the quarter and since deliveries were always quoted by

ANNUAL SALES AND PROFIT BUDGET
for the financial year ending _____

Products	Sales £	Profit £
A		
B		
C		
D	___	___
Total	___	
Technical expenses		
Selling and distribution expenses		
General administration expenses		___
Net operating profit		___

Fig. 13 Annual sales and profit budget

week number it was easy to ascertain the sales for each period. The annual budget was based on the budget for the first half-year and a forecast for the second half-year. At the end of each accounting period the actual was shown against budget and the form completed as follows:

Column 1 The annual budget figures.
Column 2 The proportion of the annual budget for the year to date.
Column 4 The budget for the period just ended.
Column 5 Actual performance for comparison with the figures shown in column 4.
Column 6 The aggregate for the periods to date. This gives a useful comparison with column 2.
Column 7 Actual performance as against the budget in column 6.

An important feature of this procedure is that any failure to meet the budget is a measure not only of loss of revenue but of the delay in executing customer orders.

capital budgets

Most capital budgets should emerge as a result of the long term planning; for example, the introduction of a new product, developing new markets, enlarging the production capacity, installing new plants and re-locating the existing plants. These considerations should all be reflected within the perspective of, say, a five-year plan. The greatest danger of the average company is to make *ad hoc* decisions on capital expenditure which deal with sections of the business in isolation. Without the guidance of a forward plan based on the most reliable information attainable showing the over-all requirements of the business in relation to, amongst other things, the product and market trends, a company has no legitimate means of deciding the importance and the priority of a project or indeed the validity of the project. Mistakes can easily be made in projecting capital expenditure. One fairly typical example is the number of companies, and even industries, that have created surplus capacity.

The need for planning capital projects against a forward plan that encompasses the total needs of the business is equally necessary for the smaller company. The experience of one company is a typical example. This company had a good profit record over a number of years but it had distributed practically the whole of it in dividends and consequently had no reserves. The plant and machinery was in good working order but two or three years earlier, machines of greatly improved design providing substantial economies in production had entered the market. To maintain its competitive position the company had to face up to a large investment in plant and since the funds available were limited this had to be spread over a period of four years.

The managing director arranged a meeting at which the executive directors, the works manager and the production engineer were present and between them they agreed the list of machines that would be purchased in the first year. The managing director mentioned this arrangement to the management consultants who were there to advise on another matter and they persuaded him, not without difficulty, to prepare a four-year plan before placing any orders for machines. The consultants were aware that there was no rationalized planning in the business—apart from an annual sales and profit budget which involved no responsibilities or commitments—and they felt that the four-year plan could be the means of introducing corporate planning in a modest way. The consultants had a discussion with each person present at the meeting for an exchange of views but concentrated particularly on the sales director finally agreeing that he should give a report of his views on products and market trends supported by certain sales statistics.

The outcome was enlightening mainly due to the report of the sales director. While all of the company's products were active some were showing a distinctly upward trend and since the production machines tended to be particular to a product line the priorities were easy to establish and proved to be quite different from the original plan.

Once the project is decided upon by top management it has to go through several stages before it finally obtains board approval. The experience of the organization in handling capital projects and the existence of properly established procedures are important factors in project implementation. Usually the first stage is to define the project in concrete terms—what it is, what it will cost and how long it will take to complete. A project aimed at increasing the output of a particular product to a given number per week may require additional space which may involve a building extension and may require additional plant and ancillaries. All of these requirements will have to be detailed and costed and the time required for implementation stated. A member of the top management team will usually be responsible for vetting and submitting the scheme for board approval. Most procedures associated with capital projects require the 'pay off' period to be stated.

The first stage in the introduction of a new product is usually (a) developing the product through drawings and sketches to a point where the production cost can be estimated and (b) an estimate by the marketing division of the selling price and the quantity that can be sold in the first, second and third years. Approval is usually required before commencing the next stage which is generally the manufacture of prototypes for market tests. The final stage, provided the first and second stages prove satisfactory, is to prepare a scheme for providing the production facilities required to manufacture the product up to a specified quantity. Other considerations may well be involved such as the average investment in inventories and marketing facilities. Capital projects are individually controlled both with regard to cost and the

P.P.C.—9

stage reached and periodical progress reports are generally submitted on major projects.

An increasing number of companies is directing and controlling the research and development division through a similar procedure. The demands on the division are translated into projects and an allowed cost allocated to each project. Where it is not practicable to estimate a cost an amount is allocated and the project is reviewed when this point of expenditure is nearly reached, when it may be cancelled or a further allocation made. It is important that all development projects of a major character should have board approval not only as a means of controlling expenditure but to ensure that the projects are given the right priority which can be a very important consideration.

Capital projects emerging from long term planning have obviously been tested for their feasibility before being released for a detailed study and report prior to approval. Top management obviously take a close interest in these projects because of the cost involved and their major impact on the future operation of the business. Many projects may be of an 'either or' nature and to protect itself against making a wrong decision where much may be at stake the average company has given careful consideration to the preparation of the form that has to be submitted for project approval. The form is designed to ensure as far as possible that all the important factors are considered in reaching the conclusion and that the 'pay off' period is evaluated. Notwithstanding the value of these procedures and the disciplined approach to project planning, top management is very much in the hands of the organization in the information presented to it for approval. In many cases the feasibility of the project may not be in doubt and the problems may lie in the manner of implementation. If, for example, the object is to provide production facilities for a new product, the competence of the production engineer in determining the manufacturing methods and selecting the plant can have a marked bearing on the quality of the implementation. In a similar manner, the figures projected as the selling price and the sales potential of a new product can influence the final decision. It is vitally important, therefore, that management satisfies itself that the persons involved are competent to provide the relevant information. It is in this area that some companies are weak; the feasibility of the project may be properly established, the procedures and the form of presentation may be first-class, but the competence of the persons actually preparing the information may be doubtful. In one case a production director signed a project form relying upon the signature of the production engineer. It transpired that the production engineer, a very competent man, whose department was operating under heavy pressure assigned the task to a clever but relatively inexperienced engineer and a serious error of judgement was made and not spotted.

The reliance of a business on its organization can be illustrated by the following example. The production engineer of a large factory sub-divided into product divisions had to consider the replacement of a substantial number of automatic machines in one division. The machines were due for replacement under an eight-year renewal plan. After exhaustive enquiries the production engineer found that the best machines available were the same make as the machines that were being replaced and that the design had not changed from the viewpoint of improved performance. Eight years without any progress was foreign to the ideas of the production engineer and after extensive consideration and investigation he introduced transfer machines which showed a satisfactory 'pay off'. Here was a case where the initiative and the calibre of the man furthered the interest of the business as he could easily have submitted a capital requisition for automatic machines and had it approved.

The approach to capital expenditure projects can be summed up as:

1 TESTING THE FEASIBILITY OF THE PROJECT Most capital projects should emerge from the long term plan and the feasibility should be tested against the total needs of the business.

2 DISCIPLINED PLANNING Procedures should be established and the presentation formalized to a point that ensures as far as this is practicable that all major factors have been duly considered in reaching the decision.

3 COMPETENCE The persons who contribute the information should be competent to make the contribution that is required from them. Reliance upon the signature of the production engineer and the production director, for example, is not sufficient unless the detailed work involved has been delegated with due regard to the requirements and the competency of the individual to undertake it.

the profit perspective

Profit has to be recognized for what it is, not as an end in itself, but as the reward for services rendered, tangible or intangible. There are several factors that can have a marked influence on the profitability of a business and these warrant special consideration.

A business cannot hope to be successful unless it has the skills and resources suitable for the products or services it provides, and given these basic requirements management has to ensure that they are applied to maximum effect. This can only be done effectively through systematic planning which sets the long term and operational objectives within the framework of the business policies, primarily the product/market policy. The operational objectives have to be translated into set tasks for executives, heads of departments, foremen and key personnel, showing what is expected from them and how their performance will be measured. Direction, administration, delegation, co-ordination and control are the key factors in implementing the operational objectives.

A business must have marketable products, or services, that can be sold at prices and in sufficient volume to enable it to operate economically. Volume is a significant factor not only for its impact on fixed expenses but for more important reasons because if this is inadequate there will almost certainly be a compromise between the best way of doing things and the way the business can afford, and this can lead to a weak competitive position. The type of business is largely determined by the products it makes, the markets that it serves and its volume of sales, and there is an optimum organization for each type of business. If a product design department is too small to encompass the skills demanded by the products or the marketing organization is curtailed, perhaps through the number of sales engineers employed, or the production engineering department is limited in its outlook by the economics of the situation, then it cannot be said that a business has the skills demanded or the optimum organization. In these circumstances a business is not soundly based and is unlikely to earn the level of profit required for successful growth. The small or medium-sized business that persists in making products that are only suited to the large manufacturer is a case in point.

Guidelines for managing the business should be incorporated in a system of management that will define the planning and operational disciplines and the principles, practices and performance standards. The management system sets a rational approach to decision making at all levels of the business. It simplifies the problems of succession, at a time when persons of outstanding ability and natural talents are too few in number to satisfy the demand, by raising the standards of performance of ordinary individuals.

The considerations mentioned are important contributary factors in establishing a business that is basically sound and operationally efficient. Given these conditions the profitability of the business will not be in doubt but it will nevertheless be necessary to conserve the resources by closely controlling the costs. Waste and excessive expenditure must be curbed, and the number of persons employed must be maintained at a planned level through a close control of recruitment. Probably the most effective control of costs, and one not always fully appreciated, is to ensure that output is up to the level warranted by the expenditure incurred.

A business must be soundly based and operationally effective or otherwise its annual profit budget cannot project a satisfactory performance. Operational planning and effective implementation can have a marked influence on the profit earned. This will be assessed and projected in the annual budget and will be tested frequently by the profit earned. The operational planning will be the basis for deciding the tactics to be adopted to improve or at least maintain the sales volume and share of the market. The trading prospects will be assessed by considering such factors as the political and economic outlook, and the impact of competition, and their total effect on the market; against this will be set the growth potential of the products and what the business has to offer. Systematic planning through planning disciplines that project an annual sales and profit budget and set individual tasks together with accountability is the best guarantee of a business attaining its objectives. No business is master of its situation and the most efficient has its good and bad years, even on occasions earning a smaller profit in a year of increased sales. The profitability of a business has, therefore, to be measured in the long term with five years as the probable minimum, and the basis of measurement commonly used is the ratio of the profit earnings before tax to the total capital employed. It is also important to ensure that the increase in profits is a measure of progress and that it represents an increasing sales volume through a larger market share in expanding product lines.

Finally the system of management accounting employed in a business is an important factor in efficient operation and management must ensure that the system satisfies the particular requirements of the business. Personal preferences can to an extent influence the system, for example, in operating a so-called actual costing system, or a conventional standard costing system, or a marginal or direct costing system. The test of the system is that it should be an effective aid to management in decision-making and in the direction, administration and control of the business.

8 management information and planning and control techniques

Before considering the planning and control techniques generally available to a business it may be appropriate to review the more important aspects of business operation as previously discussed.

CRITICAL APPRAISAL OF THE BUSINESS The aim here is to see factually what the business is and to determine what it should be and how to achieve it. The starting point is the product line or service that the business provides and its markets or customers. This prompts such considerations as: Has the product line a growth potential, or is the demand static or declining? Is the market standing of the product line—share of the market—increasing, decreasing or static? Does the volume of sales permit the business to be competitive, that is to be as favourably placed as its competitors in operating the business as it should be operated, or is it subject to the dictates of what it can afford? Is the product line or service compatible with the skills and resources of the business? This last consideration may involve a change in the product line or an extension of it to exploit fully the skills and resources of the business. Can the business see its sales income for the next three to five years in terms of its major product lines, major markets and volume?

These are fundamental and complex considerations that determine the basic efficiency of the business.

THE ORGANIZATION STRUCTURE A business must be organized for performance and should be product/market oriented. The product/market policy and the planned objectives should determine the type of organization required. The activities of the business should be carefully analysed and grouped to obtain the most effective performance. The responsibilities and duties of individuals should be clearly defined and key personnel should be allocated specific tasks within the framework of the planned objectives of the business for which they are accountable. Delegation and co-ordination should be key considerations within the framework of a management system that should permit decisions to be made as near as possible to the point of action and the facts. The maximum authority should be assigned to a position but delegation must be harnessed to the means of control and accountability. For delegation to be effective and to be extended to the lowest levels of management, which should be the aim, it must be preceded by the necessary control procedures, for delegation without control is tantamount to management abdicating its responsibility.

PRODUCT DESIGN The outstanding characteristic of every successful business is the quality of its product and there are few things, if any, that distinguish competitors more than the importance and significance attached to product design. It is in the area of product design that the greatest variety of skills converge; the marketing division establishes that there is a market for the product and lists the principal requirements in a product specification, the technical division provides the technology and innovation with close regard to economy in the use of materials and ease of production, and the production division considers the methods of manufacture in relation to the facilities available.

It is generally stated that the wants of the customer should be closely studied and that the product should cater for his needs. This is an understatement as the product in many cases has to anticipate the needs of the customer and it is this factor which makes product design so uncertain and problematical. A customer is not articulate in his wants and does not generally determine his needs; he simply expresses his preference in selecting from the products available.

Many companies could produce better products and their failure to do so does not generally stem so much from the lack of the essential skills as from setting their standards too low. Good design can be largely ascribed to 'an attitude of mind' bordering upon a philosophy, and this should be inculcated by top management. Rolls Royce is an outstanding example of this philosophy as throughout the years and through the reigns of successive managements their exceptionally high standards have been maintained. A good product is an essential ingredient for a successful business.

THE KEY FACTORS IN PRODUCTION The product line and the sales volume are the factors that generally decide the method of production. Production systems can be generally classified as: process, or flow, production which is generally applicable to the manufacture in quantity of a homogeneous product; continuous or mass production of the assembly type of product where the volume is large enough to justify machines being permanently set up to do specific operations; batch production where the volume does not justify the investment in plant warranted by continuous production; job production where the product is dictated by the requirements of the customer.

Some companies batch manufacturing the assembly type of product apply the principles of continuous production to some of their major parts by setting up a special line of machines for the specific purpose. There is no doubt that this principle could be more extensively applied in those conditions where the reduction in manufacturing costs and inventories resulting from a production line can offset the larger investment in plant.

The key factors are the type of product and the degree of standardization, the sales volume of the product and the product design. Ideally the sales volume should permit the application of the best production methods and machines. Where production engineers have to compromise between the best production methods and the economics of the situation then efficiency is impaired and a company can be at a disadvantage if its competitors are not so restricted. The design of the product is of paramount importance as it basically fixes the cost of the product. From the production viewpoint the design should minimize the production time involved in producing the product and should avoid any undue complexities. It should also give due attention to standardization to permit longer production runs. In general, companies that make standard products are alive to the virtues of standardization and practise it successfully. It is the company that makes the standard product modified to meet the particular requirements of the customer that usually fails to exploit standardization to the full and this can be further aggravated by the sales department which generally has a faculty for extending the variety of modifications, quite often beyond the real requirements of the customer. One company which was obsessed with variety to a point that production was uneconomic decided to rationalize. It made a close study of the orders received during the past year for its best selling product and found that the standard product with certain standard modifications could have satisfied 90 per cent of the orders. The sales department was instructed to offer the standard product against all enquiries at the standard delivery date and standard price; in the event that the customer required something different a higher price and an extended delivery date would be quoted. In the ensuing year the sales increased and no orders were placed for special requirements; in addition the company was complimented by customers on the reliability of its delivery dates, a condition that had not existed in the past.

There are few companies making a variety of product that are not faced sooner or later with the need for rationalization of their product lines. This may not always be apparent from a statement of product costs but it can be evident from a study of the utilisation of production capacity when the disruptive and uneconomic impact of the short production runs imposed by certain products is highlighted. In the past many companies have introduced new products with no particular policy in view and in these cases where a rational product policy is decided it is not unusual to find that in some aspects the existing product lines do not conform. Here management has to buy time as it must avoid a reduction in sales and a loss of profit however marginal. But until a business can operate a rational product policy it cannot be completely successful. A business has to be on its guard even when introducing a product that conforms to its product policy. For example one company would not introduce a new product unless the potential sales per annum exceeded a certain figure; it found from previous experience that the added burden of a new product, particularly on the production division, could only be warranted when a fixed minimum level of output could be guaranteed.

PRODUCTION PLANNING AND CONTROL In process and continuous production the key factor is to ensure that materials are available in the right quantity as and when required for production; the other factors in production planning and control are virtually built into the plant and its operation. Procurement of materials is also a key factor in batch and jobbing production but it does not end there. A feature of batch and jobbing manufacture is that common production facilities have to be used for producing the different parts and products and queuing time is, therefore, involved. A planning procedure is essential to ensure that parts are produced in the right priority and with the minimum queuing time. Two of the systems generally used for planning, particularly in the assembly type of product, are work load charts and the replacement of parts on a minimum stock re-order basis. Every part, major or minor, is given the same treatment in these systems.

It is particularly important in batch production that the production planning and control procedure is tailored to the exact needs of the business and that systems generally applicable, such as the two mentioned above, should be applied with discretion. It is easy to have too much system with ineffective control. One company that operated sophisticated systems had the idea that the production planning and control system could be made to operate so effectively that there would be no need for progressing or chasing. They persisted with this idea without achieving the results expected. Investigation showed:

1 That there was no need to operate work loads for every part on every machine. It was apparent that certain key machines were the bottleneck, or at least the limiting factor, and that production could be planned and controlled through limiting work load charts to these machines.

2 That each product included a small number of major parts and the rest minor parts. It was arranged that the major parts to be purchased would be procured against a delivery schedule previously covered by a long term purchase order. The manufacture of major parts would be planned in detail against each machine on a strict time basis.

3 That minor parts could be procured and manufactured on a minimum stock re-order basis.

4 That there was a case for a progressing function to ensure that the major parts would be procured or manufactured as planned and that the minor parts would be available to match the major parts in accordance with the assembly programme. To aid the progress function the company accepted a generous stocking policy for the minor parts.

The above procedure resulted in a reduction of total inventory, more effective planning and production control, better delivery promises, and a simplified system through recognising that the progress function had a legitimate application. The inference is that many production planning and control systems could be improved by a careful study of the needs of the particular business.

MEASURING PRODUCTION OUTPUT In process and continuous production the measurement of output is generally straightforward, for example on the weight of product produced or on the number of cars assembled. But in batch or jobbing production where there is no natural unit of output measurement can present a problem. The importance of measuring output cannot be overstressed as it is one of the vital controls in the operation of a business. Batch and jobbing work associated with engineering products often present the greatest problem. In these cases, as in every case, the volume of completed work is an important factor. Output should be planned against a weekly or monthly assembly programme and the results compared. Important as this control undoubtedly is, it is not, however, the complete story as work-in-progress and manufactured parts in stock can fluctuate, thus influencing the true volume of total output. Reference was made in an earlier chapter to the application of standard hours, the time measurement of work by the work study department, and this is the basis generally available to engineering and other types of business as the only means of measuring output.

SYSTEM OF MANAGEMENT The function of top management is to shape the business for successful growth and to direct and control its operation with profitable results. Numerically, top management is exceedingly small compared with the total number of persons employed in a business, for example five top executives for more than 1,000 employees, and in the larger business, to quote one case, seven top executives against 11,000 employees. How can so few people influence the performance of so many? Obviously management can only exert its influence on performance and the results obtained through creating the right organization and giving it direction and purpose through policies, procedures, systems of operation, training programmes and performance and operational standards. Every business has its systems of operation but few are sufficiently comprehensive to be classed as a system of management. As mentioned above management has two major functions, to plan and to operate, and a system of management has to embrace both functions. The majority of companies have systems to cover the operational aspects of the business but no established planning procedures. This gap reflects the previous concept of managements, now being eradicated, that business planning was an optional function. Progressive managements must apply time and effort to institute a system of management as without it their progress will be retarded.

PLANNING THE OBJECTIVES Planning is a unified process that falls into two categories according to the phasing of implementation, namely long term planning and operational planning. Long term planning aims at shaping the business for successful growth. In its crudest form the long term plan should determine the sales income for the next three to five years in terms of major product lines and major markets. In its more sophisticated form the long term plan generally embraces concepts as well as products. IBM sees its business in a much wider concept than simply the manufacture of computers and no doubt in its long term planning its aim will be to translate some of these concepts into new products at the earliest opportunity. But for the majority of businesses long term plans will have to be expressed in the concrete terms of products and markets. Long term plans have to be reviewed regularly and updated and dates have to be decided for implementation.

The objectives of operational planning are sales income and profit, or, to put it more precisely, the object is to shape the profit statement for the ensuing year. Management has to find the answers to the questions 'How should the business operate during the next financial year?', 'What can we hope to achieve?' and 'What tactics should we adopt to achieve it?'. Operational plans should be translated into a budget which should normally cover a period of a year to coincide with the financial year. A budget is a refinement, or an edited version, of the operational plan; it imposes operational standards with accountability for performance and it must be set with these objectives in view. A business should be able to view its prospects and decide its operational plans at least a year ahead but it does not follow that every division of a business can be accountable for performance against an annual budget. Generally the marketing, technical and financial divisions can operate against an annual budget but the probability is that the production division will only be able to operate against a shorter term budget. Where the production division cannot operate against an annual budget then the production costs should be projected against the sales budget to give management a reasonable assessment of the profit expectation and the acceptability of the budget. At this point the budget, if approved, provides the operational standards with accountability for performance for top management and all divisions of the business with the exception of the production division. The production division will be controlled through the shorter term budget appropriate to its operations. The period of the short term production budget will be determined by the period that the production division has complete control over production. If, for example, the business produces standard products the period represented by the production programme will determine the period of the budget. If the business makes non-standard products or standard products modified to meet customer requirements, it means that production can only proceed against actual orders received and here the budget period will be based on the period normally covered by the order book.

Given a business that is soundly based, which it is the object of long term planning to ensure, then the other function of management, that of operating the business can best be directed and administered through operational budgets. But it must be operational budgeting in the real sense, that is through operational standards with accountability for performance, and the production budget in particular should be related to a period that reflects the true span of production control.

PROFIT ON CAPITAL EMPLOYED Probably the best measure of the progress of a business and the one most frequently applied is the ratio of profit to capital over a number of years. The volume of sales and profit should, of course, show a progressive increase and the ratio of profit to capital employed should at least be maintained at a fairly consistent level. The sales volume should reflect the potential growth of the product line and also an increasing share of the market.

management information

Management requires information for several purposes but the main requirements are for decision-making and for checking actual performance against planned performance. Every management must be concerned with a factual approach to decision-making and ideally management must aim at obtaining all the facts. Henry L. Gantt, a pioneer of scientific management, stated the case many years ago when he said that it was immoral for management to decide as a matter of opinion what could be established as a matter of fact. The conclusive act of decision-making is intuitive; it is dependent upon business judgment and experience. There is no technique that makes decision-making automatic. Reliable data that identifies basic trends in the external forces that are likely to affect the business, coupled with a knowledge of developments inside the business, are essential aids to reaching the right conclusions.

A business has to be sensitive to the outside forces at work and take account of their probable effect in making their long term and operational plans. The outside forces may be generally classed as competitive, technological, economic, social and political. In formulating its long term plans a business may decide to ignore the economic, political and social aspects if it considers these are short term, but in deciding the operational plans for shaping the profit statement for the ensuing year these would be major considerations. In long term planning technological developments can be of primary importance because of their probable impact on the product policy of the business, but in operational planning their effect may be too long term to be taken into account.

Statistical methods and statistical forecasting are two of the most important techniques for providing management information. They use the past as a guide to the future through the various established principles and practices at their disposal including the principle of probability; they are concerned with identifying basic trends and their future implications for the business. But a business cannot plan on statistics alone without reference to current events and their probable impact on future operations. In an industry that is fairly static and not subject to any rapid change, statistics can be the determining factor in the planning of future operations, but in a rapidly changing industry the emphasis must be on current developments and their future implications. Here the need is for market intelligence related to product, customer and competition, derived from publications, contacts, surveys and market research. The astute business will tend to make use of both approaches in reaching its conclusions.

Electronic data processing systems able to deal with masses of data and to perform all the processes associated with statistical analysis at great speed will undoubtedly improve and extend the application of statistical methods in business operation.

planning and control techniques

VALUE ANALYSIS This is a technique, or discipline, that aims at cost reduction. It may be described as the systematic examination of a product, and its constituent parts, with the object of reducing the cost without affecting its performance or quality. When applied at the design stage it is usually termed value engineering and this has the advantage that improvements can be made before the business is committed to any expenditure on tools, materials and other items. Value analysis is the title given to it when the technique is applied at a later stage, for example when the product is in production; here the technique is more limited in its application since it may not be economic to introduce changes once large tooling costs have been incurred.

P.P.C.—10

Value engineering and value analysis are primarily concerned with the design and manufacture of a product and its parts. Ideally the design of a product should ensure that it functions properly, is styled to give customer appeal, and gives maximum value at minimum cost. Similarly production engineering, which determines the methods of manufacture and the tools and equipment to be used, should ensure that the product is manufactured at the lowest possible cost within the limits imposed by the production quantities. Value engineering or analysis is, therefore, not a new technique but a systematic and disciplined approach to long established principles.

It is history now but the famous Ford model 'T' was an outstanding application of the principles of value engineering and value analysis. At a time when a car was a luxury article only within the reach of a few people Ford had the idea of making a cheap car for the masses. The car had to be reliable and the selling price sufficiently low to attract the volume of orders so necessary to make it an economic proposition. As it transpired the design in its simplicity and reliability had the stamp of genius and this, backed by the production genius of Sorensen who will be remembered as the man who first introduced the moving assembly line, translated the almost incredible concept of Henry Ford into a reality.

The discipline of value engineering and value analysis has achieved some remarkable results since its introduction and has generally raised the standard wherever it has been applied. It has underlined the failure of many manufacturers to give sufficient attention to product design in all its aspects.

Many companies do arrange, of course, for the production engineers to study the design and submit their suggestions before the design is finalized. But this examination is confined to a comparatively narrow concept as the object is to simplfy and reduce the production operations, usually by easing tolerances and making minor alterations in the shapes of parts. Value engineering and value analysis have reduced the costs of products in a number of ways: substituting cheaper materials; modifying, substituting and eliminating parts; the standardization of materials and parts; the simplification and elimination of production operations.

An engineering company which used many castings made in its own foundry was concerned with the machining time involved. Following an investigation it was decided that the castings would have to be made to much closer limits, and to make this possible the manufacture of the metal pattern plates previously undertaken by the pattern shop was transferred to the toolroom which could work to finer dimensions. The result was that many castings were used without machining and the others required only a finishing operation.

Another company was concerned at the variety of its steel bars stock which covered more than 130 specifications and sizes, some of which were very expensive and difficult to obtain. Following a thorough investigation the number of varieties was reduced to 23; the most expensive specifications were eliminated and the supply problem eased, and the inventory was substantially reduced. A company fabricating a wide variety of items on a large scale was concerned with the size of its inventory and decided to make an extensive investigation. It transpired that each designer worked to his own ideas and, through the absence of a co-ordinated policy, the dimensions of the material used were often larger than necessary and there was, of course, no attempt at standardizing materials. Standards were laid down which reduced the materials cost of the products and reduced the variety and value of the inventory.

Where this discipline is introduced it is probably best to treat it as a separate function until the objectives have been achieved. Thereafter it should not generally be treated as a separate function but should revert to the functions where it properly belongs, namely product design and production engineering. The important factor is that it should be properly recognized and applied as a discipline and the design and production engineering functions should have the necessary skills to apply it.

PROJECT PLANNING — CRITICAL PATH ANALYSIS This is a technique that has been developed fairly recently for project planning in connection with construction jobs, developing new products, research and development programmes, and the like. The planning network is a graphical presentation of the activities or jobs that have to be carried out to complete the project. Some activities must precede others while some may be done simultaneously. The over-all time is determined by the longest sequence of activities, termed the critical path. The application of these planning networks has been very successful. When resources as well as activities and times are being planned and controlled the technique is called PERT.

OPERATIONS RESEARCH Operations research, first developed during the war, can be applied to many fields and one is the application of scientific methods to the solution of industrial problems. It is taking its place as a useful guide to management in decision-making where quantitative considerations and problems are involved.

Operations research makes extensive use of models—mathematical and simulation. It is scientific in that it is analytical and experimental and employs the methodologies of other branches of science. It can probably best be described through the types of problem that it is equipped to solve, some of which may be classed as inventory processes, allocation processes, queuing, sequencing and information problems.

Probably operations research has been applied more to inventory control than to any other problem. This involves several problems and one of the objects is to balance the size of the inventory against the losses that may arise through shortages of materials and supplies. Allocation is concerned with identifying the most favourable programme from a number of feasible programmes. Distribution problems are in this category and ascertaining the product-mix that will make the best use of the resources is another typical example. Queuing theory is the determination of the number of service facilities and/or scheduling arrivals. Sequencing theory is determining the order in which units awaiting service should be serviced. Information problems involve selecting the right samples to provide a reliable basis for correct decisions. Some problems involve combined processes, for example, a production control problem may combine inventory and allocation.

In the practical business setting it is likely that operations research will be complementary to, and not competing with, some of the other services or techniques such as statistical methods, market research, accounting and production engineering.

ELECTRONIC DATA PROCESSING This is probably the most revolutionary innovation in recent years. Most business concerns will have some application for a digital computer, but whether the volume of transactions and the economics justify having a computer, or hiring time on a computer, will have to be decided in borderline cases through feasibility studies. Where the transactions are voluminous and routine there is an obvious application for a computer, for example, in certain aspects of accounting, payroll preparation, inventory and stock control applications and sales analysis. This aspect of doing existing jobs better through a computer is obvious. The other aspect is obtaining information that could not be obtained economically by any other means, for example, information in connection with statistical analysis, operations research, etc. Storage facilities with the means of random access widens the scope of the computer for many jobs.

Through the years managements have complained that there are too many forms and too much paperwork in business, and the introduction of computers has provided one of the best methods yet devised of multiplying paperwork. It is obvious that much more thought and consideration must be given to the need for and the purpose to be served by each form. It is also important to decide if information should be issued as a routine or be held 'on tap' to be issued as required. Another factor that has to be emphasised is 'management by exception'. Traditionally managements have had to study a mass of information to single out the matters that required action. The computer has an opportunity here for identifying and printing out the exceptions. A case was noticed recently of a large company with a major procurement programme obtaining at regular intervals a print-out from the computer of some sixty pages showing the deliveries to date against schedule. There was no alternative but to scrutinise every item on every page to find the items that were behind schedule. This was a typical case for having an 'exceptions' print out. The logic of electronic data processing is impressive but it has yet to be matched by the thought application, or logic, prior to the computer. The information required and the form and frequency of its presentation must be logically construed to make the best use of computer time and facilities and to minimise paperwork.

MARKET RESEARCH The most important factor in management is the factual approach to decision-making: to shape the business for profit and growth through its long term planning and strategy and to translate this potential into reality through its operational planning and tactics. For most business concerns the long term planning must be directed at products, markets, share of the market, volume of sales and production capacity. Operational planning aims at adopting the most appropriate tactics to ensure the profit earnings and the financial stability of the business in the next financial year.

Management in general has a tendency to be influenced mostly by the factors which will have an immediate impact on the operating results and is thus forced into *ad hoc* decisions and operational tactics to the exclusion of long term planning and strategic decisions which in the long run present the only means of creating and consolidating a growth potential.

Strategic planning is centred mainly on the marketing view of the company's operations: 'what products, what markets, what volume of sales?'. The two services that are best equipped to provide the information for long term planning are statistical forecasting and market research; the former uses the past as a guide to the future while the latter continuously senses the marketing environment which the business through its product lines will be committed to in the future. This is an extension of the concept of market research as it is practised at present where the tendency is to use it for a specific project or survey thus applying it in a restrictive and segmentary fashion. Market research must reflect the total view of the marketing operation and must provide the complete market intelligence required by the business to audit current operations and to decide future action.

PROCEDURES In setting up planning and operational procedures management has to be aware of the planning and control techniques available and has to decide which can be usefully applied in the system of management. The well established techniques such as works study, production planning and control, and budgetary control, have been introduced in this way. In the past management has been slow to accept new techniques but this condition is changing and go-ahead managements are on the look-out for new and better methods of operating the business.

conclusions

The fundamental characteristics of the successful business do not change. The traditional concepts are as true to-day as they were in the past. The difference is that the conditions change and the increasing size of the business unit, the rate of change and the growing complexity of business operations, impose greater demands on management and the need for sophisticated information, planning, and operating techniques and procedures. It could be expected that men of genius such as Carnegie, Ford, Sloan and Leverhulme would have asserted themselves in any age. But a rapidly developing society cannot rely upon genius or natural ability, which is a rare and unpredictable commodity, for promoting its interests and the solution lies in enabling common people to do uncommon things through greater education and training and the introduction of improved techniques which although complex in their origin can be extensively applied by the relatively uninitiated.

The ultimate measure of the success of a business is, to repeat, based upon the following factors:

1 GROWTH IN THE VOLUME OF SALES A business should ensure that its product lines have a growth potential and that it is increasing its share of the market.

2 INCREASING RETURN ON THE CAPITAL INVESTMENT It is important that in the long term the profit earned on the capital investment should show an increasing trend.

3 EFFICIENT ORGANIZATION The organization should be maintained at the level of efficiency appropriate to the requirements of the business. Succession should preserve and promote the necessary skills.

appendices

appendix 1. marketing organization: notes

1 This organization chart is based on an existing organization. The marketing director operated through five executives.

2 The market research manager collected certain information on a routine basis to provide the market intelligence required by the company. He carried out special investigations, as required. He maintained comprehensive statistics compiled from the sales records of the company. He prepared questionnaires to obtain information from the sales fields, both home and export. He provided economic and market information for the annual budgets.

3 The technical service manager and his staff were organized to provide technical information to customers. This service was provided as an aid to the customer and as a means of finding new applications for existing products or developing new products.

4 The sales manager was fully responsible for all the selling activities and for sales performance. He was aided by two principal assistants; one responsible for home market sales and the other for export sales.

5 The sales office manager was responsible for orders, sales correspondence, and office records.

6 The service engineer was responsible for following up customer complaints regarding the quality of products.

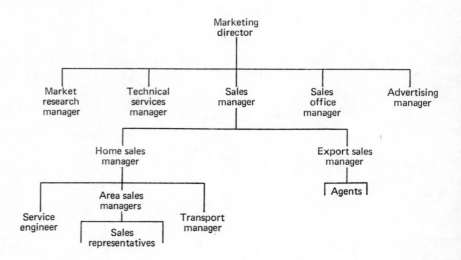

appendix 2. functional chart: notes

1 The chart shows the analysis and grouping of activities in their application to three functions; engineering, marketing and industrial relations. A similar procedure should be applied to the other functions.

2 The grouping of activities in many companies has developed through custom and practice. There is a general need for a review of these activities to ensure that they are properly organized for the best performance.

3 The first step in analysing and grouping activities is to group them first by function and then by sub-function. From this, positions can be established and the duties and responsibilities of each position can then be defined.

Illustrated functional chart of three functions

Managing director		
Director: engineering	**Director: marketing**	**Director: industrial relations**
Product design	Market research	Labour negotiations
Development	Market intelligence	Personnel relations
Drawings	Sales statistics	Standards of employment
Standardisation	Sales forecasting	Recruitment
Specifications	Budgets and programmes	Education/training
Bills of material	Advertising	Job analysis
Assembly parts lists	Sales promotion	Job specifications
Manufacturing liaison	Price estimating	Remuneration
Quality control	Pricefixing and discounts	Incentive schemes
Technical services	Selling	Personnel reports
	Distribution	Personnel records
	Orders and correspondence	Welfare
	Records	Public relations
	Warehousing and inventory control	
	Packing and transport	
	Performance standards	
	Technical services	
	After-sales service	

appendix 3. statement of responsibilities: notes

1 As a general practice statements of responsibilities should be prepared for all executives and all departmental heads down to foreman level.

2 The statement should be brief and should not attempt to outline the duties attached to each position but simply the responsibilities. It should also show the place in the organization and a reference to the organization chart (e.g. 3.2 third position, second line).

3 There should be a positive approach to the responsibilities of the position. The statement should state what the position is responsible for, and should refrain as far as possible from stating what should not be done.

4 Apart from its obvious purpose a statement of responsibilities can help a company to formulate its own views on positions and responsibilities in that it imposes a discipline leading to an organized approach to the requirements of the business.

STATEMENT OF RESPONSIBILITIES

Issue No.
Date of Issue

3.2   Production Planning Manager

A. ORGANIZATION.

   The Production Planning Manager is:
   1 Directly responsible to the Production Director.
   2 Responsible for the direction and control of production planning and control department, goods receiving and stores, and internal transport; and for all inventories for production materials.

B. MAJOR RESPONSIBILITIES.

   1 To be fully conversant with company policies, procedures, and standard practices, insofar as these relate to the departments under his control and to ensure that these are properly observed and implemented.
   2 To direct and supervise all personnel under his control; to ensure that they are adequately trained to perform effectively the duties assigned to them; to co-ordinate the work of his departments and to maintain the necessary standards of discipline.
   3 To co-operate with the marketing division in determining production programmes in accordance with sales requirements and to ensure that output objectives are obtained with the maximum effectiveness.
      (i) To prepare and submit detailed schedules to the purchasing department for the procurement of materials and parts in accordance with the delivery dates quoted.
      (ii) To prepare and submit production schedules to the production departments together with the orders and forms necessary and showing the completion

dates required; after ensuring that the production programme makes effective use of manpower and machines.

(iii) To maintain progress control to ensure that purchases are received by the due date and that production orders are completed on time.

(iv) To report to the Production Director, and others concerned, any factors outside his control which may affect the attainment of the production objective.

4 To ensure that the stores are properly laid out, and that all materials and parts are located in an orderly manner and readily accessible; to ensure that proper stock levels and re-order quantities are fixed for those items which are maintained on a stock replacement basis; to maintain the records necessary to show the current stock position; to ensure that goods are received and issued promptly and are accurately recorded on the appropriate forms; and to ensure that all storekeeping operations and routines are performed efficiently and economically.

5 To ensure that all inventories for which he is responsible are maintained at an economical level and regularly scrutinised to avoid overstocking and waste; and to issue regular reports on slow-moving and redundant items.

6 To be currently aware of the demands for internal transport and to ensure that the manpower and equipment are adequate to give an efficient and economical service.

7 To make recommendations to the Production Director for improving the performance of his department. In particular to:

(i) Make suggestions for improving procedures and standard practices.

(ii) Suggest educational and training schemes, or courses, appropriate to members of his staff.

(iii) Make periodic reports on all presonnel under his control.

8 To co-operate with other departments in providing information and services.

9 To undertake any other duties assigned to him by the Production Director.

Signed...................................

Production Director

Distribution:

appendix 4. organization chart: notes

1 This shows the whole of the organization of a business and the chart illustrated is patterned on an existing organization. It has to be emphasised, however, that each business must organize itself according to its needs and must create the organization that will give the best performance. It follows, therefore, that there is no uniformity in organization charts although guidelines can be useful as a check in formulating them.

2 The chart shown is useful as an illustration of an organization but in the larger company this form of chart could be unwieldy. The better practice is to prepare a skeleton chart showing the main functions and to prepare separate detailed charts for each function. For example in the chart illustrated only the functions and the titles and names of the directors would be given. The sub-divisions of each function would be shown on the separate chart for each function and would contain a more extensive breakdown than is given in the illustration.

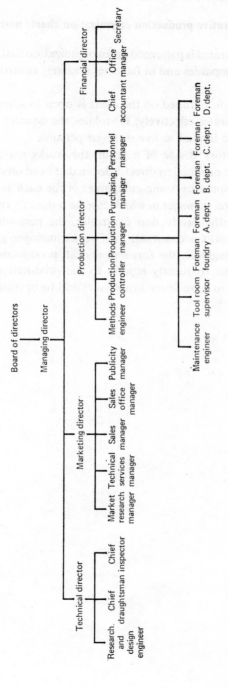

Board of directors

Managing director

Technical director — Marketing director — Production director — Financial director

Technical director:
- Research and design engineer
- Chief draughtsman
- Chief inspector

Marketing director:
- Market research manager
- Technical services manager
- Sales manager
- Sales office manager
- Publicity manager

Production director:
- Methods engineer
- Production engineer
- Production controller
- Purchasing manager
- Personnel manager

Production engineer:
- Maintenance engineer
- Tool room supervisor
- Foreman foundry
- Foreman A. dept.
- Foreman B. dept.
- Foreman C. dept.
- Foreman D. dept.

Financial director:
- Chief accountant
- Office manager
- Secretary

appendix 5. illustrative production organization chart: notes

1 The chart illustrated is patterned on an organization that is fairly common in the smaller companies and in factories remotely controlled from central headquarters.

2 The organization outlined on the chart is open to several criticisms but in practice it operates effectively. It violates the concept that the span of control should be limited to five or seven persons.

3 Where the factory is one of a group the works manager is generally responsible to the production director located at head office. An alternative organization adopted by some companies is for each factory to be controlled by a general manager in which case he is directly responsible for the works manager, the production controller, the personnel manager, the buyer and the works accountant. The works manager generally controls the production engineer, the foreman and all production personnel. The transport manager frequently reports to the production controller. It is also the practice to have fewer supervisors and to operate mainly through foremen.

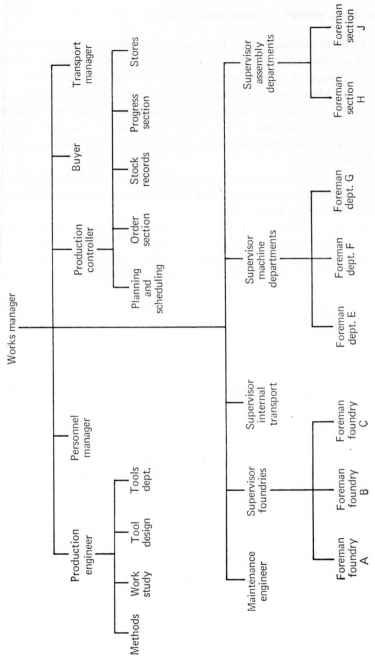

appendix 6. product explosion chart: notes

1 A product explosion chart is related to the product in the manner that an organisation chart is related to the organization; it presents a comprehensive picture of all its constituents and their relative positions.

2 An explosion chart shows not only the parts contained in the product but the time involved in producing the parts as a means of deciding the production programme. It is particularly suitable for classifying the important and the relatively unimportant parts as a basis for a selective production system.

3 The chart shows the parts necessary for final assembly together with sub-assemblies; it shows the composition of each sub-assembly and the production time of every part.

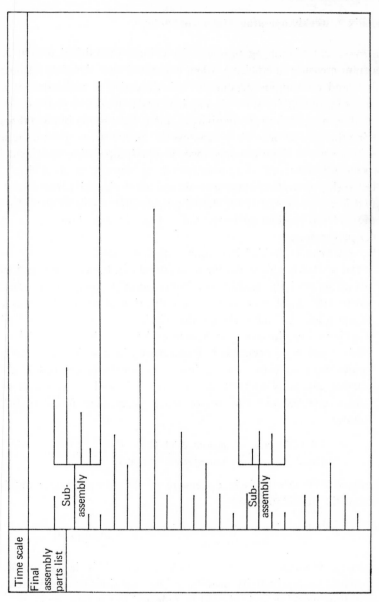

appendix 7. weekly operating statement: notes

1 In every manufacturing business the volume of finished output is an important measure of efficiency when compared with the planned output. In flow and continuous production this yardstick is self-sufficient as a measure of productivity but in the batch production of engineering products output does not measure productivity as it may have been obtained through reducing the volume of work in progress and/or the stock of manufactured parts in stores. In these circumstances a weekly operating statement is a necessary adjunct to the output statement to measure productivity.

2 The weekly operating statement shows the budgeted performance on the first line and thereafter the actual performance week by week for the duration of the production programme. The last line shows the average weekly performance.

3 The statement is divided into four distinct sections:

UTILIZATION This shows the total attendance hours of the productive operators and the number of hours actually spent on productive work. The object is to control the utilization of productive labour.

PERFORMANCE This shows the efficiency of the operator while working on productive jobs. Measured jobs are those for which work study times have been fixed. Unmeasured jobs which have no time values must be kept to a minimum as operators are not likely to operate efficiently without an incentive. Allowed hours reflect work study time values. The performance percentage is calculated as follows:

$$\frac{\text{Allowed hours} + \text{unmeasured job hours}}{\text{Measured job hours} + \text{unmeasured job hours}} \times 100 \text{ per cent}$$

PRODUCTIVITY This is a measure of the allowed hours obtained from the attendance hours:

$$\frac{\text{Allowed hours} + \text{unmeasured job hours}}{\text{Attendance hours}} \times 100 \text{ per cent}$$

GROSS WAGES AND RATE PER HOUR This is an important measure as productivity may have been obtained through excessive overtime working and this will be reflected in the rate per hour.

Weekly operating statement

Department _____
Foreman _____

Production operators: utilisation and performance   Period _____

Week number	Number of operators	Utilisation of production hours						Performance					Wages	
		Total attendance	Production	Rectific	Indirect work	Lost time	Percent	Unmeas-ured jobs	Measured jobs	Allowed	Percent	Product-ivity	Gross wages	Rate per hour
		hours	hours	hours	hours	hours		hours	hours	hours				
1	2	3	4	5	6	7	8	9	10	11	12	13	14	15
Budget														

appendix 8. a measure of output

Many companies have the problem of finding a suitable yardstick for measuring output where there is a variety of product using common production facilities but no natural unit of output. In these circumstances standard hours are widely used for measuring and controlling performance but are not satisfactory as a measure of output as they make no distinction between the costs of the different production facilities used. The standard hour in conjunction with the cost of the particular equipment used is, therefore, an answer that should provide a fair representation of output in most circumstances. Where machines are involved the standard hour rate is calculated for the machine but where it is assembly or bench work it is expressed as a rate per standard labour hour.

There is nothing new in machine hour rates but the tendency has been to include expenses which influence output but are not directly related to it, for example, indirect labour and supervision. As a measure of output only those expenses directly related to it are included in the rate. Form A shows one type of form that can be used for calculating the standard hour rate for machines and direct labour.

The following points have to be noted with regard to the form:

1 The rates are calculated for a group of similar machines unless there is only one machine of a type.

2 The rates are calculated at three volume or capacity levels, normal (or economic) volume, expected volume for the year, and the maximum volume.

3 The hours are assessed on an annual basis, and on one, two, or three shifts, according to the prevailing practice in the industry. The operating hours should preferably include machine setting time.

4 Establishment charges, or buildings expense, include depreciation and maintenance of buildings, rates and insurance, heating and lighting; all applied as a cost per square foot of space occupied.

5 The standard hours are, of course, based on the allowed times fixed by work study department.

Form B summarizes the information collected through Form A, to show the results for the factory as a whole. The total cost shown is suggested as the measure of output or volume.

Appendix 8
Figure A   Direct cost per standard hour

Number of machines	Group number	Description of machines, bench, or assembly work	Floor space	Horse-power

			Normal volume £	Expected volume £	Maximum volume £
Partly variable costs					
Labour cost					
Supplies					
Tools					
Power					
Miscellaneous direct charges			——	——	——
Total					
Fixed costs					
Depreciation plant					
Maintenance					
Establishment charges			——	——	——
Total cost			——	——	——
Cost per standard hour					
Operating hours					
Number of operators			——	——	——
Number of working days in the year					
Number of hours worked per day			——	——	——
Total working hours in the year					
Less breakdowns, etc.			——	——	——
Total operating hours					
Total standard hours					

- -

Appendix 8   Production output
Figure B   (Based on total direct production costs)

1 Description	Group number	Normal volume £	Expected volume £	Maximum volume £
Transfer machines	1			
Transfer machines	2			
Automatic machines	3			
Automatic machines	4			
Capstan machines	5			
Capstan machines	6			
Milling machines	7			
Gearcutting machines	8			
Gearcutting machines	9			
Drilling machines	10			
Tapping machines	11			
Assembly	12			
Total		——	——	——

bibliography

SLOAN, ALFRED P., JUNIOR, *My Years with General Motors*, Pan Books, London. The author was the chief executive of the company for many years and in his book he describes the growth of General Motors and outlines some of the principles and policies that contributed to its success.

BOWER, MARVIN, *The Will to Manage*, McGraw-Hill, New York and London. This book describes the management principles and applications that are essential for business success, and as managing director of Mckensey and Company, the international consulting firm, the author writes with authority on the subject.

The Accountant's Cost Handbook. Edited by Dickey, R. I., Ronald Press Company. This is a useful reference book for executives, accountants and management at every level who are concerned with budgeting, pricing policies or manufacturing costs.

SHAW, L. W., *Management Information and Statistical Method*, The General Educational Trust of the Institute of Chartered Accountants in England and Wales. A useful and concise introduction.

BURNSIDE, J., *Value Analysis*, British Productivity Council. An explanation of the technique and its applications for the guidance of executives and others.

RIVETT, PATRICK, and ACKOFF, RUSSELL I., *A Manager's Guide to Operational Research*, John Wiley, New York and London. A useful introduction that will enable executives to appreciate its applications.

BATTERSBY, ALBERT, *Network Analysis for Planning and Scheduling*, St. Martin's Press, New York.

index